MONEY AND EMOTIONAL CONFLICTS

BOOKS BY DR. EDMUND BERGLER

Frigidity in Women (in collaboration with E. Hitschmann)
Talleyrand-Napoleon-Stendhal-Grabbe
Psychic Impotence in Men
Unhappy Marriage and Divorce
Divorce Won't Help
The Battle of the Conscience
Conflict in Marriage
The Basic Neurosis
The Writer and Psychoanalysis
Money and Emotional Conflicts
Counterfeit-Sex
The Superego
Fashion and the Unconscious
Kinsey's Myth of Female Sexuality (in collaboration with W. S. Kroger)
The Revolt of the Middle-Aged Man
Homosexuality: Disease or Way of Life?
Laughter and the Sense of Humor
The Psychology of Gambling
One Thousand Homosexuals
Principles of Self-Damage
Tensions Can Be Reduced to Nuisances
Curable and Incurable Neurotics
Justice and Injustice (in collaboration with J.A.M. Meerloo)
Parents not Guilty!
Selected Papers of Edmund Bergler, M. D.: 1933-1961

Money and Emotional Conflicts

BY EDMUND BERGLER, M.D.

International Universities Press, Inc.

First Printed by Doubleday

Library of Congress Cataloging in Publication Data

Bergler, Edmund, 1899-1962.
  Money and emotional conflicts.

  Reprint. Originally published: Pagent Books, 1959.
  1. Money—Psychological aspects. 2. Conflict
(Psychology) I. Title.
RC569.5.M66B47   1984   155.9′2   84-22390
ISBN 0-8236-3445-0

Manufactured in the United States
of America.

A HUSBAND: "I want you to teach my wife the beauty of thrift."

PSYCHIATRIST: "Do you mean the necessity or advisability of thrift?"

HUSBAND: "Not at all. I mean the beauty of thrift. There is something nice and sentimental about thrift. A dollar is a dollar."

PSYCHIATRIST: "That is mathematically correct."

HUSBAND: "There is more to it in thrift. Beauty, do you hear me, real beauty . . ."

Verbatim excerpts from a consultation in the office

CONTENTS

FOREWORD TO SECOND EDITION

When the present book first appeared in 1951, it
elicited a long series of friendly reviews, and—disappeared from the book market. Neither the rate of
sale nor the initial continuity of sale warranted a
second printing.

In the last few years, requests for the neglected
work have multiplied. It seems that time weakened
the public's resistance to it. Inquiries about the out-
of-print title, directed both to bookstores and to
the author, have steadily increased. Ridiculous
prices have been paid for second-hand copies.

Why did a book on "money neurosis" (a term
denoting misuse of money for unconscious purposes) not make a greater impression "saleswise,"
despite good reviews? Was a cynical editor justified
in stating: "The trouble was in the title; you should
have named it 'How To Make More Money By
Using New Psychology'"?

There are two types of taboo in the book business: the conventional taboo and the inner taboo. The former refers to topics "one does not talk about"; the latter variety is officially harmless, but impinges on the sacred belief of the reader that he "knows all about it." Obviously, my book interfered with that second, temporarily immovable set of prejudices. The situation therefore remained uninfluenced, even by favorable reviews, most of which cautiously° singled out specific sub-chapters such as those on gambling and bargain-hunters. To name a few samples: "Often lively, witty and entertaining" (NEW YORK TIMES); "Full of clever insight and full of surprises for the layman" (BOSTON TRAVELER); "Original, entertaining and authoritative stuff by a highly qualified psychoanalyst who can talk plain English" (OAKLAND, CAL. TRIBUNE); "An overwhelming book" (WORCESTER, MASS. TELEGRAM); "Offers a superb analysis" (PITTSBURGH SUN-TELEGRAPH).

Samuel Johnson averred: "There are few ways in which a man can be more innocently employed than in getting money." That "innocence" also reduces itself to the assumption that "smartness" alone (or lack of it) determines the individual's monetary success (or failure). The statement that *inner* obstacles can prevent a man from being thus "innocently employed" contradicts one of the basic beliefs of the average person. This apparently self-evident tenet, which amounts to an unwarranted prejudice, is being challenged in the following pages. This accounts for the inner resistance to this information: nothing is more tenacious than a popular myth. Still, complacently reducing complex psychic phenomena to the formula, "A dollar is a dollar," does not solve problems—at least, not those that have unconscious connotations.

EDMUND BERGLER

New York City, January, 1959

°The topic proved so unfamiliar to some reviewers that in rare cases where objections were voiced, those were on the level of misunderstandings. E.g., one reviewer objected to the stress laid in the text on inner self-damaging tendencies, calling this "oversimplification of human aspiration." Underestimation of psychic masochism, however, is in my opinion like playing handball with an atomic bomb. Another reviewer rescued himself into humor: "The author writes: 'Gambling is a neurotic disease requiring psychiatric treatment.' A couch, perhaps, beside every broker's telephone . . ."

FOREWORD TO FIRST EDITION

The general approach to money matters is full of contradictions. We say that "money isn't everything," but the "successful" citizen is admired and respected. This lack of uniform standards results in one person calling extravagance what another labels stinginess.

The majority of people, however, take for granted that everyone wishes to make money. Ask yourself, when you laugh at a joke about niggardliness, whether a note of admiration may not be included in your laughter. For instance, when you laugh at the expense of the Scotchman who bargains with a farmer over the price of a single cucumber half ripe on the vine and who, after long haggling, succeeds in purchasing it for a penny, stipulating: "Don't cut it off; I'll call for it in a fortnight"—are you enjoying yourself only because of the absurdity of the Scotchman's stinginess or do you admire his bargaining power as well?

None can deny the importance of money for the individual in our society; only a neurotic will make a shibboleth of it. The not-too-neurotic person will try to make money as best he can and as extensively as he can. But he will not risk jail or sacrifice his individual happiness—health, love, hobbies, leisure, or contentment—to do so.

The purpose of this book is to investigate the *unconscious* reasons, *secondarily* connected with money, which cause a specific disease: *"money neurosis."*

Money neurosis has many masks—from stinginess to success hunting, from gambling to gold-digging parasitism, from impostor-like features to bargain hunting. In short, *anything* can be used by neurotics as hitching posts for their inner conflicts. Money is *one* of these hitching posts.

Money neurosis can be found in every country, every culture, every group of any given society; therefore it cannot be used to prove anything against our system of free enterprise. For money neurosis is a by-product arising independently of any external system. Hence, any attempt to adduce, from this purely scientific investigation of a specific group of neurotics, arguments to be utilized in current ideological, political, and economic fights is hereby stigmatized as unwarranted misuse. Psychoanalytic psychiatry has neither reformatory, political nor propagandistic aims. It describes unconscious motivations and resultant inner defenses of the *individual* neurotic, works out psychological remedies for the *individual* neurotic, recommends and performs *individual* treatment, and ends its work at exactly that point.

Money neurosis, in one sense, simply proves the ingenuity of neurotics: confronted with prevailing values, they use them for defensive expressions of repressed infantile aims. *Neurosis is ageless and timeless;* the manifestations and the use of "raw material" merely vary in different cultural and economic orbits.

New York, March 1950   EDMUND BERGLER

PART ONE: THE PSYCHOLOGICAL PROBLEM OF MONEY

Money, which represents the prose of life, and which is hardly spoken of in parlors without an apology, is, in its effects and laws, as beautiful as roses.

RALPH WALDO EMERSON, *Nominalist and Realist*

1. THE NORMAL AND NEUROTIC APPROACH TO MONEY

In most societies money represents a definite and concise reality value. As a medium of exchange it is capable of purchasing specific and actual objects and specific and actual services. No one can honestly deny its importance, but money can be used for neurotic purposes. It is at this point that the psychological problem begins.

During the period in which his individual psyche is being formed (from the start of extrauterine life up to the age of five) the child has no precise conception of money. Hence, money has a meaning for the individual only later in life. The money neurotic is one who secondarily shifts the values stemming from the nursery to money. If, for instance, a child of two and a half desires the exclusive possession of a doll and wages a fierce struggle with a sibling for the toy—does the child think of the dollar-and-cents value of the doll? And again, if the same child becomes furious because the mother shows more attention to a younger brother—does the child want the exclusive possession of the love and attention of the mother because it thinks of the insurance "value" of the mother as expressed in dollars? The answer to both questions is, of course, no. Yet this greed for exclusive possession can, after some psychic detours, be shifted later in life to money, and such a child can develop into a miser jealously guarding his purse strings.

Does this mean that the wish to amass money is the result of an instinctual drive to possess? Not at all. Such a drive does not exist. What is clinically observable in the child is childlike megalomania: ideas of grandeur and omnipotence; he is the center of the entire universe. Bit by bit this fantasy is destroyed by reality and the child shifts from the first objects of admiration to others and still later to inanimate and impersonal objects, like money. Without understanding the ideas of omnipotence which every child harbors, the understanding of the neurotic roots of the greed for money becomes impossible.

Psychoanalytic psychiatry, created by Freud, unearthed the fact that the child's "adaptation to reality" is not alone a process of learning something *new;* more decisively, it implies the destruction and overcoming of something *old,* namely, the highly irrational fantasy of omnipotence. All adults are familiar with the complete dependence of the newborn and the fact that without adult care the infant would inevitably die of hunger or exposure. The trouble is that the infant does not know it and lives on the basis of the illusion of omnipotence. This illusion is based on fact: the sheltered existence in the womb, where food and oxygen were provided automatically. To regain this lost paradise is the infant's fight after birth. Neither babies nor adults give up preferential positions without putting up some kind of a struggle.

As later neurotic manifestations prove, the baby follows a definite course of actions: first, it ignores disturbing reality and pretends that nothing has happened and scotomizes radically changed conditions; then, when ignoring does not help, it mobilizes aggression and cries furiously. To complicate matters further, in the first few weeks of the baby's life, the parents of necessity prolong the intrauterine situation: most of his time is spent wrapped in a warm quilt sleeping in a darkened room. The parents are not responsible for the fact that the baby must now inhale and exhale air, and suck and swallow milk (two exertions spared the unborn). Every time the child awakens, milk is given to him.

Such a situation fosters in the child a misconception of his own "autarchy." According to this simplified outlook on life, the child is an omnipotent sorcerer: he awakened, he cried, and at that signal the bottle magically appeared out of nowhere and entered his mouth. Thus, the child gives everything to himself out of himself. The child takes no cognizance of the outer world; somewhat later, when the outer world inevitably makes its presence felt, the child mistakes it as an object brought into being by his own omnipotence. He stretches out his hand toward an object and his mother hands it to him. That is what actually happens, but the child's belief is that he has reversed the roles: he has given a "magical sign" and the mother is but the executive organ of his omnipotence. He has given himself the object.

The child's fantasy of being omnipotent constantly comes into conflict with reality, one painful experience after another teaching him the fallacy of his assumption. But instead of relinquishing the fallacy in face of the reality, the child merely shifts it. First parents, then teachers are considered omnipotent. When these assumptions also collapse, omnipotence is shifted once more, this time to Fate. The child has a very personalized relationship to his own projections. He behaves as if it is only he whom Fate watches and guides. These feelings have both positive and negative connotations. The unconscious formula runs something like this: "If I'm not omnipotent, at least I am capable of forcing people (Fate) to give me *exclusive* love, attention, and admiration." The fantasy of original omnipotence is rarely if ever discarded; it is discernible even in the fearful masochistic type: "Fate is watching with great interest every step I take, even if it punishes me."

The unconscious denominator of both ramifications of shifted omnipotence is: "*I* create my admiring and guiding Fates (or punishing watchdogs). *I* have and possess them; they don't own me. They are *my* executive organs."

Therefore, the first cornerstone of the urge to possess is a compensatory mechanism the purpose of which is to heal a wound to the child's self-love, his narcissism. This, then, is the reason why the so-called instinct to possess does not exist; an instinct is an inborn drive and not a defense mechanism.

All children are helpless and dependent. All children, at first, try to deny and negate that dependence. Sooner or later the normal child inwardly makes the necessary adjustments to the subjects of his dependence (in the cultural family—mother, father). The neurotic child, however, does not. *One* of the innumerable neurotic solutions,[1] one which is of importance in the problem of money neurosis, is *unconscious stabilization on the rejection level.*

Under the term stabilization on the rejection level, I understand the fact that the neurotic child clings to his libidinous-aggressive demand of exclusiveness projected upon the parents and the resultant automatic disappointments, which, in turn, are unconsciously accepted not *despite* but *because of* the accompanying displeasure. For example, a child asks its mother for some candy. The mother refuses, perhaps for some dietetic reason. Now imagine this same child some twenty years later, standing before the window of a candy store and staring with hungry eyes at the display. That grown-up child, now a full-fledged

[1]The whole development of the libidinous-aggressive tendencies of the child in the pre-oedipal and oedipal periods is, of course, more complicated. The reader is referred to my book *The Basic Neurosis* (Grune & Stratton, N. Y., 1949), which summarizes analytic controversies on this topic. In the present volume I have concentrated with deliberate one-sidedness on only *one* facet of the problem. See also *The Superego* (Grune & Stratton, N. Y., 1952).

neurotic, let us say, instead of walking into the store and buying as much candy as he desires turns his back on the window and walks away. What has occurred unconsciously? Obviously, for this type of neurotic, the showing up of the mother as the great disappointer is dynamically more important to him than the wish to get.

A man once made an appointment for the express purpose of consulting me about the conflicts in his marital life. His first words upon taking a chair were: "I hate you!" Even in a psychiatrist's office this is a rare opening, and I asked if we had ever met before. He denied that we had, and gave as a reason for his "hatred" the following explanation:

A few years previous to his visit he had read a book of mine dealing with the problems of neurotic marriages. This book's main thesis is that there are no innocent victims in such a marriage, that unconsciously two neurotics look for and find each other. While reading, the painfully disturbing thought occurred to him that were he in analysis with me, I would claim that he was by no means an innocent victim of his "shrewish" wife as he believed, but had unconsciously selected and married her for the express purpose of "being kicked around." For three years this one thought had made his life miserable. Finally he decided to find out if his suspicion was justified, and therefore was now sitting in my office.

In trying to arrange the fee for treatment, the man offered to pay half my usual fee and was deeply indignant upon my refusal to accept his proposition. It turned out that he harbored the grotesque idea that I owed him something for having disturbed "his peace of mind."

Did this man really want treatment? Obviously not, for I never heard from him again. A truly psychic masochistic *provocateur*, he had arranged the consultation for one reason and one reason only—to make sure that I, the author of the book which had painfully disturbed him, would be "unjust" to him.

We call people who are unconsciously stabilized on the rejection level *psychic masochists*. Their love of disappointments is not conscious. On the contrary, on the conscious level they are angry, bitter, complaining, and accusing. This is the surface manifestation the world sees, and the reason it sees it is because the inner conscience of a psychic masochist constantly accuses him of "unconscious pleasure," which in this case happens to be displeasure. To counteract the unconscious accusation he furnishes an inner defense: *I* am angry and refusing.

In studying the life histories of these neurotics, one finds that their whole emotional energy is spent in the unconscious construction and concoction of situations in which they are disappointed.

How does such a fantastic distortion of feelings arise? How can anyone in the world desire unhappiness, refusal, and disappointment—more than desire it, enjoy it? The answer is to be found in a duality of factors: the already described fantasy of infantile megalomania *and* the unfavorable position of the child's only defensive weapon, his inborn aggression. Unlike most animals, the human being has a long and protracted maturation time. At the same time his *drives,* at least potentially, *are present from birth in the strength of the adult's.* Every time infantile megalomania is offended by the refusal of a libidinous wish, fury appears. To use a simple example, the baby awakens and wants to be fed. The minute or two before the mother can fulfill the wish mean nothing nutritionally, but from the standpoint of offense to the child's megalomania the delay may be disastrous, one of the thousands upon thousands of disappointments leading to the final collapse of the fantasy of omnipotence. The child's crying gives one the impression of *helpless* fury. As the child grows, this helplessness is further accentuated by the weakness of his muscular apparatus (to feel the full fury of a man in rage and to have nothing to punch with is the exact position). With this inadequate apparatus the child encounters the punishment (physical or nonphysical) meted out by the giants of the nursery. Still later, he meets the moral embargoes imposed on all naughtiness and stubbornness when they are directed against the mother and father.

Finally, after the inner conscience is built up, inner guilt enters the scene and that triad of retribution—punishment, moral reproach, guilt—under favorable conditions is strong enough to convince the child that a diplomatic adaptation to the commands of the parents is necessary. In such a case, aggressions are shifted to less holy people than parents, changed, modified, and sublimated. The end result of such an adaptation is relative normalcy.

But if a child does not follow the above pattern, unconsciously clinging instead to his original megalomania and fury against parental authority, the result will be trouble—psychic masochism.

One of my patients, a schizoid personality, prided himself on being what he called an "independent person." The only use he made of this so-called pride of independence was that with boring regularity it brought him into self-provoked conflict with his superiors. During his analysis the department in which he worked was combined with another and subordinated to a new vice-president, a man whose politeness was reputed to cover great conceit and who was known never to forgive an offense. Shortly after the combining of the two departments, this superior gave a party in order to become acquainted with his new staff. He greeted my patient in a friendly manner and apologized for an oversight of the day before.

"I almost didn't recognize you on the street yesterday," the vice-president said, "but please try to understand that it was only because lately I've been introduced to so many new people."

To which my patient, stout masochist that he was, promptly replied: "I understand. In such cases *I* hold with the advice I read once in a book of Ehrenstein's. The author confesses that he had such a low opinion of people that in order to make himself a civilized being he greeted all the dogs he met on the street politely; after some time he devaluated his greetings to the dogs to such a degree that he was capable of greeting all his acquaintances without any difficulty."

Naturally, at the first opportunity, my patient was fired.

Quite naturally, too, for weeks after my patient filled my office with his wails of the great injustice done him, and the meanness and brutality of the vice-president.

Seemingly, it never occurred to the patient (until the incident was analyzed) that he, knowing full well the boss's reputation, had deliberately provoked him and placed himself and his job in jeopardy.

Psychologically, every human being lives on the basis of "pursuit of happiness." Every human being desires happiness and the avoidance of pain. To make this formula work, the psychic masochist performs a fantastic task. Unconsciously he must learn to extract "happiness" from very real unhappiness. The problem is solved by starting to *like* punishment, moral reproach, and guilt. By sugar-coating pain with a libidinous layer, the principle of "pleasure in pain" is unconsciously established. At this point the paradoxical formula *"The only pleasure one can derive from displeasure is to make of that displeasure a pleasure"* has found a new adherent. All psychic masochists are unconsciously self-created.

Unconsciously, the psychic masochist is a glutton for punishment and derives a double pleasure out of being refused—the pleasure of pain and the pleasure of maintaining alleged infantile omnipotence. The latter is decisive, for the moment punishment is accepted, omnipotence is triumphant. The abstruse unconscious formula is this: that fool believes that *he* kicks, deprives, and refuses me; quite the contrary. He is just an executive organ of *my* omnipotence, since, through my initial provocation, *I make him* kick, deprive, and refuse me. Needless to say, all this peculiar reassuring takes place below the level of consciousness; in the psychic masochist's[2] conscious mind he desires love, warmth, and approval. But "unexplainably" he receives always the one thing—refusal. That this refusal is unconsciously *self-chosen, self-created,* and *self-perpetuated* is not known to him consciously.

In some neurotics the tendency to "collect injustices" is so marked that anything may be utilized for this express purpose. The elevator of the building in which my office is located was, for a period of time, closed off because an automatic car was being installed. In the interim all passengers had to use the service

[2]Unconscious *psychic* masochism should not be confused with *perversion* masochism. The latter denotes *conscious* acceptance of bodily pain as pleasure.

car in the rear. A woman patient of mine became very interested
in the switch-over and made specific inquiries of the building
employees about the progress of the work, the costs, etc. Still,
every time she had to use the service car, she felt that I had
forced her to do so "only to degrade her." Thus we see how easily
a neurotic can manufacture affront. These neurotics "transfer"
their unconscious feelings toward the original alleged malefactor
of their nursery to the people who surround them in their adult
life. And never for one second is the neurotic *consciously* aware
of the pattern.

The life of the psychic masochist is further complicated by the
fact that the neurotic "solution," once established, has to be
maintained against constant and renewed reproaches from the
inner conscience. The latter begrudges and objects to the peculiar
type of pleasure achieved by the so-called solution. Therefore,
new defenses have to be constantly furnished. This new and
secondary defense is the fiction that the neurotic himself is but
the innocent victim of people's meanness and cruelty. The neurotic sufferer trades on the ever-ready aggression of his fellow
man. Having once achieved the latter, he fights it unsuccessfully
and pities himself, claiming that terrible injustice has been done
him and that "it could only happen to poor little me." The masochistic schedule operates constantly and invariably along the following prefabricated lines:

(1) "I provoke (or misuse) a situation in order to be refused.
(2) I do not see that I provoked the situation and I am simply
confronted with the other fellow's aggression, which I fight
energetically in self-defense and in righteous indignation. (3) I
pity myself because of the terrible injustice done me."[3]

The neurotic approach to money is a *specific case* of the previously described masochistic triad. One must realize that a person burdened with the masochistic solution of his nursery conflict unconsciously lives all of his adult life *exclusively* on the
basis of *pseudo-aggressive defense.* By hook or crook he must

[3]This triad has been first described by the author, and named the
"mechanism of orality." For details see *The Basic Neurosis.*

convince his accusing conscience (and himself) that he is not a masochistic weakling. He tries to achieve this more or less hopeless aim with the exaggerated play-acting of aggression (pseudo aggression).

This pseudo-aggressive act, performed to appease the accusing inner conscience, manifests itself in two ways: refusal to part with money and accumulation of money.

Every demand for money seems an accusation of passivity; in other words: Were I not considered a wishy-washy sort of a person, they would not dare to ask for it. The excitement of such neurotics, when confronted with a demand or request for money, activates the latent reproach and its inevitable defensive result: the hyperaggression in refusal. All of us have witnessed such hyperaggression, and, to date, no one has logically explained why, in cases like this, a simple and detached "Sorry, no" is not deemed sufficient to deny the request for money. No one has explained just why the whole scale of fury has to be put into psychic operation.

The reason is probably that to refuse money demands or requests means, for the sufferer from money neurosis, not what he *consciously* believes (the triumph of not being a sucker) but *unconsciously*, and therefore much more decisively, the aggressive refusal furnishes the badly needed alibi of not being a *passive masochistic weakling*. This seems the crux of the matter.

The second unconscious pseudo-aggressive defense, presented to the inner conscience, is, of course: "I don't want to be refused, I want to accumulate and to get."

In the miser, for instance, we see both defenses at work at the same time: the unwillingness to spend and the frantic need to accumulate. In doing both, he clings desperately to his pseudo-aggressive defense on an unconscious level. The real battle of stinginess, however, is not fought with dollars and cents. The real battle of money is fought intrapsychically from the reservoirs of unconscious guilt and unconscious defense mechanisms.

All physicians are conscious of the fact that some of their patients have an irrational and rebellious attitude toward the payment of medical bills. This rebellion against the paying of doctor's bills represents an unconscious recapitulation of the anger engendered at the giving up of the most cherished fantasy of childhood, that of alleged omnipotence. Confronted by the physician, *everyone* (including the physician himself when he is ill) changes into the helpless and frightened child. This child-in-the-patient projects upon any chance physician in moments of crisis his *own* infantile megalomania, and in this manner attributes to the doctor magical powers. Thus, all physicians can observe in their patients two quite contradictory attitudes: the eager and trusting confidence bestowed beforehand and, quite often, the ever ready devaluation afterward.

All the silly rationalizations encountered in patients who refuse or are reluctant to pay medical bills (Health is something so precious it should not be measured in money, or, A physician should be ashamed to think about money) are just *emotional objections against the successive bearer of the old but never worn-out fantasy of childlike megalomania.* For these people the payment of a medical bill means, *unconsciously: payment and support of a competitor who remained in the business while they themselves were forced out of it.*

Another emotional element is the unconscious identification which the patient makes with his physician on the basis of "identical etiological claims" (Freud): they are both specialists in omnipotence, and why pay money to oneself? It is amusing to observe that some of the most conventional people often show this irrational mode of behavior where doctors' bills are concerned. They take pleasure in making the doctor wait for his money, or they demand smaller bills, and some of them even cheat their doctors. There is one exception to this form of behavior, and even then magic is once more involved. Strangely enough, these are the patients who are overly prompt in paying their doctor's bill; in most cases, they do so because they are afraid of the doctor's magic power of revenge. They pay quickly in an unconscious sense of appeasement and the desire to avoid his magical wrath.

Still another element plays a part in this strange money relationship. The first people concerned with a child's health are his parents; but when an adult is confronted with a physician who must be paid for his service the whole infantile resentment against "not being loved" enters the picture. Whoever heard of parents asking for money when their child is sick? In other words, being pushed into the situation of a child in sickness causes a conflict in the adult centered about the never-abolished wish to be a child. One could say that the emotional infantilism brought to the fore by adult illness is one of the last rebellions of the neurotic adult.

In the course of the years I have had many patients afflicted with money neurosis, which, as I was their physician, was quite aggravated in their money contacts with me. There was the one wealthy woman who always insisted on taking some of the time from her costly appointments to sit at my desk and make out a check for her bill in order to save a three-cent stamp. A man once insisted upon paying his monthly bill in dimes, a practice he immediately ceased when I started to count them on his time.

Besides many other difficulties, another patient suffered from a complete lack of self-criticism. He never made a joke directed at himself, but he was witty so long as he could prove his superiority by deriding other people. He was very touchy and deeply offended, however, if others joked about him. This brought him into continual social conflict. Hence I suggested analyzing his lack of humor. The patient thought it over carefully to see whether some reasonable return could be expected, then solemnly and a bit pompously offered his considered opinion. "You are mistaken. I have an excellent sense of humor, but I cannot afford to amuse you at the prices I am paying here." When I burst out laughing, the patient was surprised; he did not see that he had made a joke. Money was for him no joking matter.

I remember still another patient who would appear five minutes late for his appointment and turn his watch back five minutes. When I asked him to explain his behavior, he first denied manipulating his watch, then admitted it, giving the following excuse: "I'm not stingy, as you believe, nor am I trying to cheat you or provoke a situation of injustice claiming that you cheat me. I just don't want you to have the satisfaction of getting your money without working for it.".

Then there was an accountant who was recommended to me by a general practitioner with whom he discussed at great length the terrible expense of analytic treatment and my fee specifically. Finally he consented to the fee and entered treatment. One month later, on receiving his bill, he maintained that I had made a mistake and charged him double. He believed that the fee per appointment pertained always to *two* appointments. When I told him that as an accountant he must have known better, he said quite seriously, "I always buy two pair of shoes, two trousers, two neckties—everything wholesale—why not two appointments?"

Perhaps the longest battle was with the parent of another patient, and it could easily have resulted in serious consequences. The very wealthy father of a neurotic daughter was faced with the fact that the young lady needed psychiatric treatment and needed it badly. He belonged to that category of fathers who believe that after giving their children an expensive education parental duties are over. He consented reluctantly to treatment for his daughter, only after having ascertained that a sanitarium would be more expensive. Not knowing that I knew this, he hypocritically told me that he would do anything in the world for his daughter. The agreement we reached involved payment for treatment and an allowance to his daughter until she was capable of working again. A conflict began almost immediately after the start of treatment, the father adamantly refusing to pay the full amount of the stipulated allowance, using as an excuse the statement that the treatment was much more expensive than he had ever dreamed. This was at once serious for my patient, as she became antagonistic to treatment, believing that I, indirectly, was responsible for the smaller allowance. I tried to convince the family that the original agreement should be kept, and received the following message from the father: "If you are such a humanitarian, why not reduce your fee for the girl's benefit?" I offered to reduce the fee ten per cent on the condition that the money saved would be added to the patient's allowance. "Nothing doing," was the immediate answer. "We need the money for ourselves." Whereupon I advised them that they must allow me to tell the patient the facts of the case. "Go ahead; we don't care," was the final reply. Knowing her family's approach toward money, the patient was not surprised at my disclosure. Treatment proceeded, and the next running conflict was constant demand for further reduction of the fee. Finally came the father's ultimatum: "Either you reduce your fee fifty per cent or we interrupt treatment immediately!" I refused to be bluffed and asked whether he wished me to suggest a colleague as his daughter was still quite ill. Seeing that the bluff did not work, the family gave in. But never once in the long battle did the father give any intimation that he thought of his daughter as anything but so much money going down the drain.

These are but a few examples from a long list; every physician can supply one just as long.

A further proof of the fact that neurotic tendencies come first, and the misuse of money for exactly these neurotic tendencies only much later, can be adduced from the shameful, rather barbaric patterns of some neurotic mothers and fathers. Out of quite logical expectations of inheritance, they have made a bargaining point for the purpose of imposing their whims and their presence upon their adult children. Through the course of the years I have analyzed many neurotics with the "inheritance complex." One patient, a woman, called the attitude of her mother "emotional parasitism." At first glance, the complaints of this neurotic group sounded reasonable enough. They had mothers (these were in the majority) who acted as if their sons, daughters, sons- and daughters-in-law had no life of their own but were born for only one purpose: to please them, to cater to them, and to suit them exclusive of all others. The patients' complaints were all similar in content: extraordinary demands for companionship, the parents' presence in their homes, or vice versa, the constant demands for time, the need to adapt one's taste and opinions and mode of behavior. Frequently they reported that the big stick (the last will and testament) was shaken in their faces. Said one such victim of his mother's "emotional dictatorship": "I have either to post-

pone my life until my mother dies or renounce my inheritance."
All my patients of this type were full of bitterness and fury,
nursing with deep indignation each and every new imposition on
their privacy.

Analysis of these people proved that a specific distinction has
to be made between the reality state (the demands of the older
monied generation) and the *neurotic misuse* of this situation.
Many aging mothers are neurotic and irrational in their demands
upon their children. The normal person realizes this, and also the
fact that nothing can be done about it, and makes the necessary
adjustments to the situation. But this is a far cry from the pseudo-
aggressive outbursts so frequently heard from neurotic grown-up
children.

The counterpart to the dictatorship of monied parents is the
attitude of some grown-up children whose parents depend on
them for financial support. Neurosis works both ways. This type
makes their parents feel their dependence.

It cannot be stressed too often that the *ability to absorb and
neutralize unavoidable injustices* is one of the signs of relative
normalcy. In the reverse, the masochistic pitfall of misusing these
very real injustice situations is a purely psychological problem.
No one denies that there are plenty of injustices around—there
are.

To state the case in general applicability: Relative normalcy is
an automatic absorbing of unavoidable injustices, which are externally and internally rejected. This neutralizing attitude of
"making the best of it" does not lead to a slavelike submission: one
fights for one's rights at the exact moment when the struggle
makes sense and has a fighting chance of success. The neurotic
approach is exactly the opposite: an automatic seeking-out of
avoidable injustices, and also a misuse of the unavoidable ones,
turning them into tragedies instead of demoting them to nuisances. Both types of injustices are internally welcomed and
sought out. The external rejection is not for the purpose of elimi-
nating the injustice, but an ineffective pseudo-aggressive act to
supply an alibi for the benefit of conscience. The latter, wise to
the trick, has to be hoodwinked by alibis and pseudo suffering.

Hence, in pseudo aggression, we find the choice of weapons, or method, or timing of the fight ineffective. These methods kindle the fire instead of putting it out.

Every neurotic harbors what I call an "elastic fraud corner."[4] Basically, it represents remnants of the old megalomaniacal idea of "being an exception," as Freud named it in another connection. Having suffered so much, such an "exception" can allow himself (or so he believes) to cut corners with respect to the usual moral requirements. The fraud corner is elastic and frequently given to rather fantastic stretching, which, in turn, *produces masochistic results.*

Hence, the *tendency* on the part of every neurotic to cheat in money matters. This does not imply, of course, that every neurotic acts incorrectly in his handling of money; it does mean, however, that every neurotic has, to a quantitatively differing degree, that tendency. It does not pertain to the neurotic's conscious correct self, but to the dissatisfied infant in him (repressed and invisible), who has to produce his pseudo-aggressive alibi. Whether or not this tendency is put into actual operation in money matters depends on many internal and external factors. In any case, it explains why, at times, even our most correct people act, let us say, "peculiarly" in matters concerning money.

Before closing this general chapter on the psychic mechanism of money neurosis and going on to the analysis of specific groups, it might be well if the reader had some sort of a "behavior" chart as a guide. As has been shown, there is a definite difference, in adults, between the normal and abnormal approach to money. Simplified, the difference is this:

Normally, money is a means to an end, that end the acquiring of things one desires.	*Neurotically,* money is an end per se.
Normally, one does not allow himself to be taken advantage of in money matters, and will do his best to avoid it.	*Neurotically,* the fear of being taken advantage of in money matters is greatly out of proportion to the threat itself.

[4]First described in *The Basic Neurosis,* p. 145.

Normally, one tries to make money as best he can and as much as he can, but in the process will not sacrifice either health, love, hobbies, recreation, or contentment to this end.

Neurotically, money becomes the center of life; everything else —health, love, hobbies, recreation, and contentment—is subordinated to the urge to possess it.

Normally, money has no infantile strings attached to it.

Neurotically, money is a blind for existing and repressed infantile conflicts.

Normally, the spending of money is taken for granted; it needs no surgical operation to put a dollar into circulation.

Neurotically, the possession and hoarding of money becomes the predominant motif.

Normally, unjustified demands for money are warded off (out of necessity) in a matter-of-fact way.

Neurotically, demands or requests for money generate fury, excitement, and indignation.

Normally, the phrase "I cannot afford it" is a simple statement of an objective fact.

Neurotically, the phrase, "I cannot afford it" represents a defensive triumph against psychic masochism.

PART TWO: THE SUCCESS HUNTER

The child's first impressions nearly always deeply influence psyche and personality, and frequently become permanent for the whole life.

Preface to Prince de Bénévent's (Talleyrand) Memoires, written in 1816, published by the Duc de Broglie.

2. SIX PLUS ONE SAFEGUARDS IN JUDGING SUCCESS AND FAILURE

General opinion holds that success consists of a combination of two factors—personal initiative and impersonal luck. True, the successful man exaggerates the importance of the first ingredient, and the unsuccessful that of the second. If one is to believe the man at the pinnacle of success, he is reaping the rewards of productive ideas that have come to him "in a brilliant flash." The unsuccessful citizen, however, will say that such a man was simply lucky.

Attempts at separating the unit, initiative and

luck, are not new. "Throw a lucky man into the sea," goes an old oriental adage, "and he will come out with a fish in his mouth." The opposite extreme is expressed in Chatfield's epigram: "Good and bad luck is but a synonym, in the great majority of instances, for good and bad judgment."

Stressing the element of luck, and thus minimizing the part played by personal merit in success, is the revenge of the failure. Mark Twain perfectly expressed this sour-grapes attitude in his ironic formula: "All you need in life are ignorance and confidence, and then success is sure."

The old quarrel over the quantitative admixture of merit and luck in success overlooks a *third* and decisive factor. That factor, *absence of inner obstacles to success,* has never been stressed, and could only be completely understood with the advent of modern psychiatry. Neurotic disturbance of the third and decisive part of the triad of success results in the prevention of shrewd evaluation of external possibilities, of consistency in following through, and even, in many cases, of the very emergence of the "brilliant idea" at the right moment.

It might be assumed that the person seeking success wishes himself well and hopes wholeheartedly for the attainment of the goal. Unfortunately, the assumption would be false, since there exists in the human psyche a deterring element which works to prevent success. This self-retarding element is unconscious, hence not under conscious control. Call it what you will—unconscious self-damage, gluttony for punishment, or psychic masochism—this third element has been proved, by clinical experience, to be responsible for the majority of failures.

The opinions of the average person are arrived at by processes of simplification and what we may call pigeonholing: phenomena are complicated and confusing until simplified and labeled. The result of these comforting processes is—simplified and nicely labeled error. And having established the simplified labels, the next step toward achieving peace of mind is a stabilized measure for judging others. The yardstick most commonly employed bears the tag: success or failure.

This double technique of warding off the threat of complications from things one does not understand and people one cannot fathom rounds out contemporary thinking processes. It is a useful approach; the only trouble is, it leads to wrong conclusions.

The success-and-failure yardstick is as simple as it is deceiving. Many a criminal scheme is successful—until detected. According to the simplified view, the criminal promoting the scheme is a success so long as he stays out of Sing Sing; on the day he is caught, he becomes a failure.

However, the facts of success and failure cannot be ignored. They enter, inevitably, into everyone's judgment of himself and others. The average, financially-not-too-successful man has moments of suspecting that there is something wrong with him, otherwise why isn't he more successful? He judges others by the same standard. Therefore it is important to establish safeguards to insure that the yardstick of success and failure may mean something in judging people.

One element too frequently overlooked in the judgment of success is inner contentment. The man at the top may have spent all of his time and energy in getting there; often his emotional life is withered, he is burned out and old beyond his years. On the other hand, the little man may have led a relatively contented emotional and family life.

This is not to say that lack of ambition is a guarantee of contentment; there are happy men among those who have achieved great worldly success as there are bitter and unhappy men among those who have not. One thing is clear: every individual must be judged according to his own emotional needs and expectations.

No less important is an investigation of the reasons preventing success in many success-hungry and gifted people. Edison's formula for success in the field of invention—10 per cent inspiration and 90 per cent perspiration—can be amplified psychiatrically. It is possible to define inspiration, to determine when and why it makes its appearance and to explain the origin of the wild energy and the consistency necessary for the follow-through process. It is possible, too, in some cases, to release the hidden and still unproductive energy of the future successful man.

Many people believe that, given a formula for success—no tiresome explanations or deductions, just the formula in as few words as possible—they can do the rest. Unfortunately for the impatient, the formula is of no value without an understanding of its meaning.

We live in an age of definitions and semantics. What is the definition of success? Was Hitler a success or a failure? A failure, obviously. But for years this paranoiacal gangster appeared to be a great success. The answer lies in the fact that true success contains an element of *stability*. The Third Reich, Hitler promised, would last a thousand years. Its actual duration was twelve years, for six of which Germany was at war. Hitler's goal was world domination; what he achieved was utter destitution for the master race.

What about such men as Hitler's brothers-under-the-skin Capone and Dillinger? Could either of them be called a success? Prison and the morgue, respectively, point to the answer. Yet each had a certain initial success in amassing money and power. Apart from the moral issues involved, the Prohibition outlaws were failures; true success, in addition to denoting something of stability, is never in jeopardy through the *taking of chances (prison, social disgrace) that endanger an integral part of a plan.* At the height of temporary success, the Prohibition gangsters of the era took just such chances—and lost.

There are men who, after long years of failure, achieve a weekend success only to lose, by some stupid mistake, all they have won and to return to obscurity and poverty. Others, after repeated success, fail temporarily, later recouping. Success cannot be judged except by studying a *cross section of a man's life.* Fleeting misfortunes for the successful and transitory pseudo victories for the failure prove nothing.

No remarkable feats are expected of the man who lacks initiative, but it is natural to wonder why an apparently vital and energetic person does not succeed. Success has, in actual fact, some connection with the *inner elasticity and activity of the individual.*

No one thinks it strange that in times of deep economic depression even the gifted person is temporarily down. Neither is there anything odd in the fact that a new invention may put the manufacturer of an outdated product out of business or that a man cannot become chief engineer of an atom plant without a specialized knowledge of technical engineering. Common sense tells us that in judging success and failure we must *consider the man's opportunities.*

The obituary of the man who has worked himself to death in his efforts to amass wealth might be: "The fool! What did he get out of life?" When one utters this familiar judgment he is using the yardstick of *inner contentment.* Success, then, means more than fame or money in the bank; it must not impair life's normal contentment, or, for that matter, life itself.

Now we have six initial guideposts for judging success and failure:

1. *Stability.*
2. *Avoidance of prison and social disgrace.*
3. *Cross section of a man's life.*
4. *Man's inner elasticity and activity.*
5. *Consideration of man's opportunities.*
6. *Inner contentment.*

At this point *the unconscious enters the picture.* The next, unconsciously determined, guidepost we will distinguish by calling it, not simply the seventh guidepost, but *six plus one.* Perhaps this will serve to give it a suitable impressiveness, as in the old story of the wise man who suggested that a sign in a train be changed from: "It is positively forbidden to leave the train when in motion" to: "Jump from the train in motion—and see what happens to you."

The *unconscious* that is so widely mentioned and even more widely misunderstood is *the state within the state* of your Ego, invisible and all-powerful. Objections to this statement are inevitable; one *must* meet them with skepticism—the unconscious itself has seen to that by installing within the individual a series of deterring factors to prevent his comprehending its power. That power rests, in fact, precisely in the situation described: a situation comparable to that of public opinion in a dictatorial state where it, the public, gets only the news which suits the dictator. The dictator has no objection to the people's forming "opinions" so long as those opinions are based exclusively on the facts he permits to be circulated.

And, like the dictator, the unconscious allows its slave to imagine that he is free to make decisions—and even to find his own rationalizations for carrying out the tyrant's commands: this last is, in fact, the slave's only "right."

A patient of mine, the mother of a boy of two and a half, reported the following incident. The child, who cannot yet read, was looking through The New York *Times* when he came across a page containing many pictures—the obituary page. Immediately he expressed the wish that his mother print his picture on that page so that everybody would look at him. The mother patiently explained that only *dead* people of some importance achieved that sorry spot, whereupon the boy burst into tears and complained that his mother did not love him, since she wouldn't co-operate with his wishes. True, the boy will learn soon enough the undesirability of death, and become acquainted with the limitations of parental power and influence, but at the time he could not be convinced that his mother was not simply and unreasonably refusing to grant his wish. And in that moment the misjudgment that prompted the statement, "You don't love me," may have become embalmed in his unconscious.

These misconceptions are caused by, first, the infantile megalomania which leads the child to assume that he has only to express a wish to see it carried out as if by magic; second, by the fact that objective rules of conduct, when explained to the child, are believed by him to be tricks to divert him and to disguise, hypocritically, maternal refusal; and third, by the fact that someone else must be responsible: in this case, the mother.

What is constantly misunderstood and underrated by adults is the fact that *intellectual* growing up does not automatically include *emotional* growing up. People may be divided—making a broad generalization—into two classes, those who overcame infantile fantasies and misconceptions to a great degree, and those who overcame them with markedly less success. The first group is euphemistically known as "normal," the second is called "neurotic." The difference between the two is but a few degrees of irrationality, more or less. Both grow up to adulthood—physically and intellectually. Neither any longer *consciously* demands the impossible.

What happened to the irrational part of the child's psychological make-up—his infantile fantasy of omnipotence, his wish for exclusive love, his tendency to blame his mother and father? The educator might say that these impossible, absurd unconscious fantasies and wishes were overcome in the educational process. Unfortunately, the psychiatrist, who sees a good number of these educational successes in later years, has a different story to tell. The power of the educator is less impressive than he believes; some children make a reasonable adaptation to reality and some do not, though the educator has acted indentically in both cases. He has tried through various educational media—love, kindness, persuasion, the offering of himself as a model for identification—coupled with reward, punishment, and the implementing of guilt, to impress on the child certain rules governing civilized conduct. It follows that education (and the word is used in its widest sense) is but one determining factor in the bringing up of children. In the triad of influences—biology, education, and *the child's unconscious reactions to both*—the third mysterious influence seems to be predominant. Were this not so, later instituted psychiatric therapy could not remodel the neurotic, and that such change is possible is, of course, a matter of clinical record.

The child's wishes center around the triad, megalomania, libido, aggression. Libido in the infant means the pleasurable irritation of mucous membranes. The mucosa of the mouth, employed in sucking milk and later tasting solid food, transmits, via the nervous system, a series of pleasurable stimuli: we speak of "oral libido." Later, other organs are endowed, in the process of their unavoidable use, with libido: hence the terms anal, urethral, phallic libido, etc. In puberty these subdivisions are concentrated under the primacy of the genitalia, although the original depositions wrest a good-sized portion of the psychic energy.

Aggression in the infant simply means activity, and this includes crying, spitting, vomiting, attempts at use of the muscular apparatus.

Megalomania, libido, and aggression appear in mixed proportions. The sequence of events is always the same: a child feels some libidinous urge and gives one of his magic signs. Since he is still living on the basis of autarchic megalomania, every delay deeply offends this most cherished fantasy of the infant, and the offense, in turn, in addition to real or fancied frustration, produces fury and aggression. The aggression comes into conflict with the stronger environment; it is held in check by the triad of retribution: punishment, moral reproach, guilt. The handling or mishandling of the conflict is the decisive step in the personal history of the individual. One child adapts himself to reality; another chooses the "pleasure-in-displeasure" pattern of psychic masochism.

To further complicate matters, whichever solution the child finds, it is contradicted by his inner enemy, his unconscious conscience. The term *battle of the conscience* describes that tragic section of antihedonism in the personality. And this battle of the conscience brings countermeasures to the fore: *the battle of alibis*. The result of these two intrapsychic battles is that unconscious wishes per se never make their appearance. Defenses do— and *only* defenses.

The key to psychological misjudgment of people is this: it arises from confusing unconscious wish and unconscious defense. In order to judge correctly it is necessary to understand that the identical unconscious tendency can produce many different clinical pictures. Herein lies the layman's misunderstanding. The objective facts are that the number of unconscious *wishes* in general can be counted on the fingers of one hand, whereas the number of *defense mechanisms* (meaning "inner alibis") runs into the thousands.

The term success must be qualified if confusion is to be avoided. Success may be *moderate,* or it may be *spectacular—* the word moderate here being used solely for purposes of differentiation and not in any deprecatory sense. The man who makes a decent living, supports his family, loves his wife, his children and his hobbies, and has normal social contacts and interests—in short, is relatively content—has achieved success in life. But the seeker after spectacular success has only contempt for this kind of success. He is after big things—big money, dazzling fame; he yearns to be in the limelight, admired and envied by all. This type of man we shall designate *the success hunter.*

The phrase, "Let the best man win," when used in sports, means that there are no hard feelings involved and that objective facts will be allowed to decide the issue. But in the business world the best man is assumed to be the man who has achieved the greatest amount of success; success is identified with superiority, failure and relative failure with inferiority. This is, of course, fallacious. The moderately successful man is not "inferior," nor is the success hunter propelled by "superior" aims based on greater intellectual power.

The average person intuitively chooses the way of contentment. He works when forced to, and not too hard either, if he can help it. He makes, if possible, a decent living, and lives a relatively contented family-and-hobby life. Great "ambition" is foreign to him; he is not plagued by the disturbing driving power of the success hunter. We are not concerned here with this normal businessman but with the seeker after spectacular success *who is driven by an unconscious conflict into his "ambition."* The success hunter did not consciously select his ambition, and if he wins out in his unconscious self-cure, he does so because the balance of inner powers made it possible. Frequently he pays for his ambition with a lack of inner contentment. It is superfluous to state this deduction is not meant to be an apology for inactivity and "lack of ambition." Activity is normal and necessary for the normal person.

The relative "happiness" of the average person and the success hunter have entirely different sources. The pleasures of the former are more solid, corresponding to modifications of his real unconscious wishes. The *apparent* self-love to be observed frequently in the latter has as its aim, in inner reality, the refutation of a reproach by his inner conscience.

I'm just too good-hearted for this cruel world.

Statement by a failure patient

3. EXCUSES FOR FAILURE

Psychic masochism is a universal phenomenon: every human being carries a good-sized amount of it. But the bearer of this unconsciously pleasure-coated self-damaging tendency has no inkling of the fact. An unconscious mechanism is—unconscious, and there is no bargaining possible with what is consciously unknown. If modern psychiatry had contributed only this one simple fact to the understanding of human actions and reactions, it would have done more for the elucidation of the psychic apparatus than was achieved by the combined efforts of all the philosophers of all preceding centuries.

There is—understandably—a tremendous resistance to the idea that one harbors within him a strong tendency to self-damage. Confronted by failure, people in general follow a set pattern of excuses: their competitors are cruel, ruthless, mean; or times are hard. They themselves are unlucky, even jinxed. Everything from cut-throat competition through unfortunate external circumstances to impersonal fate is mobilized in defense. Everyone and everything is accused—except one's own self-damaging tendencies.

Let us examine one of the more common excuses for failure: human malice. This can be disposed of speedily—it is not a valid excuse. People *are* often malicious, cruel, merciless. They may be, where self-interest is involved, after another man's scalp. But that man, when he complains of the scalping, is confessing to a remarkable miscalculation: why wasn't he prepared for such a possibility? What reason had he to believe that competitors, or even disinterested onlookers, would give him a helping hand? Harsh though it may sound, the realistic fact is that in the business world the precept "Act decently and others will be decent too" rarely applies. As a bitter patient once said to me: "The nursery alphabet starts with A; the adult alphabet also starts with A, but there is a word attached to it—Aggression." Regrettable, but true.

Every adult over twenty who has not acquired some conception of the darker side of human nature is automatically *suspect of cultivating naïveté for the purpose of being disappointed.* It is a common masochistic trick to take an overoptimistic attitude toward others in spite of past experience having proved such an attitude unjustified. In this way the glutton for inner punishment prepares for himself a greater disappointment, and then when he has got what he was after—a kick in the jaw—he whimpers that in this rotten world you just have to expect the worst, a condition which he implies is completely foreign to his kind and benevolent nature.

It is not my intention to negate the quality of human decency. Decency exists; it is by no means an illusion. But the neurotic conscience of many people is elastic enough to permit them all too often to behave ruthlessly, without human kindness or consideration, toward others. It is necessary to face that fact and to recognize the situation in which one's own consideration will not be reciprocated. True, people rarely know enough about the other fellow to guess whether, where, or how he punishes himself for his impossible behavior toward them. Often the aggressive offender gets his own share of kicks in another sector of his life—which is small comfort to those whom he has damaged. On the other hand, to declare that *everyone* is to be distrusted is equally fallacious. Therefore, psychological insight in human contact is no luxury but very necessary.

To return to the common excuse for failure, the second one, blaming hard times, brings instantly to mind the question: why were these hard times not foreseen in the original calculation? Sometimes, of course, reality factors do actually interfere with the carrying out of a plan. The safeguard against misjudging this type of failure, the yardstick which indicates whether the failure was normal or neurotic in origin, is simple. People cannot be judged by the outcome of one single venture. The question is whether they make failure an episode or a permanent station in life.

All these excuses refer to a wide variety of realistic *and* neurotic factors. Experience proves that not all ventures can be successful; a great many obstacles are unpredictable, and external events beyond one's foresight and control may prevent success. To be clearly distinguished from these *unavoidable* factors are those which are predictable on the basis of clear thinking uninfluenced by internal self-damaging tendencies.

Frequently what appears to be objective judgment is from the start disguised psychic masochism. It is not to be expected that every plan and hope will materialize; actually, one out of ten is a favorable average. But if *all* one's plans miscarry, not for short periods but over a span of years, something is wrong.

Psychic masochists have many seemingly different ways of coping with their inner problem, but most of these are unproductive and may be lumped under the heading of "injustice-collecting." Of the few productive solutions, one is the at least externally successful solution of the success hunter. He is demoniacally driven to the creation of his particular defense mechanism against the reproach of inner conscience pertaining to masochistic passivity. This inner defense results in success. But he pays a terrific price for his self-cure. Often it seems a case of the remedy being worse than the illness, though this, of course, is not always visible at the surface level.

In the normal person, self-assurance prevails in spite of temporary failures. His psychological mechanism may be compared to the mechanism of those dolls which, however you push or throw them, always revert to the upright position. Hope—and not, as in the case of the neurotic, pessimism—does actually spring eternal in the breast of the not-too-neurotic average person. This is not to say that the normal individual is full of naïve optimism; on the contrary, he is rather skeptical. His attitude might be described as one of "skeptical optimism," meaning that he knows, as we say, what the score is in regard to people, situations, and hard facts.

A patient in the late forties, a man in the theatrical business, suffering from a severe obsessional neurosis, was faced with the following situation requiring immediate decision. He and a partner, a man without theatrical experience, had leased a theater and were looking for a suitable play. My patient had been in show business for thirty years, had had many ups and downs (more of the latter than the former, by the way), and was entering the new venture with great expectations. His partner had invested a good deal of money, but his own investment was small and he had achieved the partnership only because of his reputation in the theatrical field.

Three plays had been submitted. The first was a melodrama by an English author about a husband deliberately driving his wife into psychosis. Our specialist rejected this play immediately and without the slightest hesitation because he disliked such plots. To my surprise, the man who could not make up his mind in trivial matters—more, suffered from "obsessional delirium"[1]—

[1]Freud's terminology.

spoke, in this case, with absolute conviction and without even traces of ambivalence. When I pointed out that his reasoning was too personal, based on his neurotic fears, he admitted it, but at the same time declared that his judgment was objective and soundly founded on thirty years of experience. His arguments were that few husbands could identify with the hero of this play, that psychiatry was too farfetched a method of getting rid of one's wife, that women would object, anyhow, to even the mention of such a possibility, and that, since the recipe was bad, women would force their husbands to reject the play as immoral. The melodrama later became a big hit on Broadway and ran for three years.

The second play submitted was a musical comedy, the music for which had been written by a composer who had died a few years earlier. "No good," was the patient's immediate decision. "It's a revival, and the first performance years ago was a flop. People never revise opinions of that kind—especially critics. Once a flop always a flop." He brushed aside my suggestion that the aversion underlying his reasoning might be connected with his neurotic fear of death, especially in view of the death of the composer. (The patient's fear extended even to the obituary page, and for twenty years he had not read newspapers because his favorite, The New York *Times*, printed editorials opposite the death notices.) "There's no need to get too personal about this," he said. "I have my objective reasons." Ironically, the musical comedy also became a hit and ran in another theater for two years.

The patient finally decided in favor of the third play, a rather weakly dramatized detective story produced by a man with whom, previously, he had had conflicts based on the latter's "impertinent and highbrow manner." The contract stipulated cash returns, with the actors' salaries paid first. The play was more or less of a failure and performances were continued on a basis of hope and little more. The result was that the producer lost no money but my patient and his partner did. More important was the loss of prestige for the patient, who had guessed wrong three times. The outcome for him was guilt, reproach, and the bitter knowledge that he was a laughingstock to his competitors.

In evaluating the patient's actions we need not dwell on the obvious aspects of his neurotic behavior—his self-damaging tendencies, his projection of inner conflicts upon reality, and his masochistic submission toward the insolent producer. Equally clear is the fact that his unconsciously masochistically intended decisions were superficially covered up with aggression: he took great pleasure, consciously, in rejecting, and in playing the big shot. We shall concentrate on one problem exclusively: why did this man *not* hesitate in making and executing his neurotic decisions, when typically he was torn by ambivalent indecision even in trivial matters? What was the sequence of events preceding the execution of the first impulse?

It was obvious that the patient's masochistic Ego, when confronted with the problem of a really far-reaching decision, made an *instantaneous* masochistic decision. The conspicuous absence of ambivalence in such a case was caused by *the unconscious certainty of failure and resulting self-damage, which provided even more unconscious pleasure than ambivalence in dosi refracta.* The masochistically pleasurable indecision was relinquished for, so to speak, the infinitely more alluring predictable failure.

In little things the patient was, to quote him, "swallowed by indecision." In one of his many unhappy affairs with women, the course of which I was able to observe in analysis, the sequence of events was as follows. I quote the patient: "After talking with the girl for a few minutes I got the impression that she was mentally unbalanced. My first impulse was to leave her alone, forget her. Afterward I questioned the correctness of my first impression and continued the relationship, full of doubts." Here we see that the first impulse was one of normal self-preservation and avoidance of trouble. The self-damaging tendency entered the picture and was acted on later, on second thought. Studying the first impulses of this patient, I concluded that he always acted masochistically, in matters both big and small. In important decisions, however, the first impulse was always instantaneously masochistic, without ambivalance, whereas in un-important decisions the first impulse was dictated by normal self-preservation, only to be reversed on second thought because of masochistic ambivalence. The end results were identical, since in both instances he acted masochistically.

The normal laws of morality do not apply to me.

4. THE SUCCESS HUNTER'S COMMON TROUBLE: LIVING ABOVE EMOTIONAL MEANS

Mortality statistics show a high percentage of big businessmen dying in the early fifties of diseases which, if not promoted by, are at least exacerbated by, chronic excitement—heart troubles, vascular diseases, high blood pressure, perforated ulcer, etc. A common belief is that business, with its worries and vicissitudes, causes these premature deaths, but this is putting the cart before the horse. The truth is that his specific excitement craving pushed the success-hunter businessman into a field that is undeniably laden with problems of tension, responsibility and competition, and that the same psychic constitution causes him to find these problems exciting to an often fatal degree.

Observing the big businessman at work, one frequently gets the impression of tension out of all proportion to the real stakes. For a man engaged in a small business, or employed in a small capacity by a large concern, to worry about survival is understandable enough. But why does the big businessman react to situations involving not security but simply greater expansion and larger profits with as much excitement as though life itself were at stake? The irrationality of his behavior is explicable only if one understands the type habitually encountered in big business.

This type, the success hunter, is characterized by the following ten "symptoms":

1. Contempt for moderate earnings, high-pitched ambitions, and exaggerated ideas of success, combined with a drive to overwork.

2. Constant inner tension, stemming from inner passivity, regardless of the importance of the stakes.

3. A propelling impetus toward more and more success.

4. Dissatisfaction and boredom if deprived of new business excitement and resulting opportunities to show off.

5. Cynical outlook, hypersensitivity, and hypersuspiciousness.

6. Contempt for and ruthlessness toward the unsuccessful.

7. One-sided and opinionated I-know-better attitude in general.

8. Hypochondriacal worries: doubts concerning continuous flow of ideas and luck.

9. Inability to enjoy the simple pleasures of life.

10. Hidden depression, warded off with tempered megalomania and extensive air of importance.

These ten points require some elaboration:

One, *contempt for moderate earnings, high-pitched ambitions, and exaggerated ideas of success, combined with overwork.* The world in general sees as a mere matter of ambition the difference between the man who is content with a moderate income and a relatively happy life with his family and hobbies, and the big businessman constantly striving for more and more money and power. Unaware of the psychological facts, people attribute this mysterious ambition to some inborn and enviable drive—at the same time rather inconsistently believing that ambition can be artificially promoted: otherwise why are we the recipients of so much advice, both spoken and written, urging the unambitious among us to cultivate more ambition?

In reality ambition is an unconsciously determined attitude which cannot be instilled by good advice, prodding, cajolery, or even self-determinism. *Ambition, if exaggerated, constitutes an unconscious defense mechanism.* The inner enemy to be warded off is repressed masochistic passivity. It might be thought that abundant activity could manifest itself as real, not compensatory, ambition, but clinical facts prove that this is not the case. Normal people spend only a particle of their emotional energy on reality aims; the greater part is spent in the enjoyment of family life, hobbies, and such other activities as contribute to life content-ment. Not so the success hunter. No slave laboring under the whip of the slave driver ever worked harder than the neurotic under the whip of inner necessity to furnish inner defenses for the placating of his inner conscience.

Businessmen often pride themselves on their enormous capacity for work, having nothing but scorn for those who, in their eyes, waste time. Stressing efficiency, meticulous attention to detail, and iron consistency, these people boast of the driving energy that they consider the key to their individual success.

Work is a psychologically complicated phenomenon. The *punitive* character of work was recognized, intuitively, in very early times: it is written in Genesis that Adam and Eve, expelled from Paradise, were forced to work as a punishment for their sin. Work has other connotations as well: it may be narcissistic, exhibitionistic, a deposition of energy and activity, an instrument for the pleasure of achievement (proof of activity presented to the inner conscience), even sublimation of unconscious libidi-nous tendencies. Unfortunately only a small minority of people are free to choose their work voluntarily, the condition under which inner wishes have the greatest chance of being sublimated. For the majority, work is only a dreary necessity for the purpose of making a living, and to them the mysterious phenomenon of a man who likes his work—one of those happy few with freedom of choice—presents a picture either of hypocrisy or of an individual with a peculiar taste for unimaginable pleasures.

Work is, among other things, an offense to infantile megalomania. It is introduced to the child as a duty, and every duty coming from outside is in contradiction to the child idea of grandeur. Education tries, of course, to sugar-coat the bitter pill, but with little success. *Dolce far niente,* the pleasure of doing nothing, remains the ideal of most people, though guilt stemming from conscience prevents their admitting it. Work is the way in which the average person pays off his conscience; in the evening he is usually in a good mood because, having done a day's work, he is free to indulge in more enjoyable activities.

Hence overwork done under the disguise of ambition is generally a case of toiling for conscience's sake. But even this fails, as a rule, because the pressure of inner demand is so great that even after an exhausting day of overwork the ambitious person spends sleepless nights tormented by business worries.

The *low* work efficiency of many people, occasioned in part by conscious motives of rebellion against insufficient wages and the monotony of their work, is chiefly due to the problem of work as an offense to infantile megalomania. This results in an expenditure of energy out of proportion to the amount of work accomplished, with subsequent feelings of physical depletion. Obviously to do a small amount of work requires only a minimum of energy; therefore the constantly observed and truly tragic tiredness of these people at the end of a day's work cannot be the result of the effort involved. It is, in fact, but the psychosomatic expression of offense to infantile megalomania.

One of the tragedies of protracted infantile megalomania, partly fostered by education, is that the child's megalomania is capable of being more or less inhibited. If the inhibition is less, the results are ambiguous: the individual has a happy-go-lucky attitude—so long as things go his way, but confronted with serious reverses, he collapses more easily than the individual whose megalomania was more severely inhibited. Of course, education per se does not do the damage; there are many educators who successfully steer a course between too much and too little love, freedom, and attention.

The success hunter, driven by his inner need to provide alibis disproving the Super-Ego's accusations of passivity, not only uses overwork as the chief of those alibis but—because he is not conscious of that fact—looks with contempt on those lazy people who lack his ambition. It is an ironic picture to contemplate.

The second of the ten symptoms characterizing the success hunter is: *Constant inner tension, stemming from inner passivity, regardless of the importance of the stakes.* The businessman's inner masochistic passivity—the constant tension of which he complains—shows a Janus face: on one side success, on the other death. Or, to put the matter less dramatically, his alibi against this masochistic passivity pushes him on to success at the same time that it literally wears him out.

"I'm glad I entered analysis *after* I'd achieved business success," remarked a clever patient of mine. "Otherwise, I'm afraid I'd never be able to pay your fee. Without my neurotic defense I would be a fifty-dollar-a-week clerk."

"You are mistaken," I said. "Assuming you had entered analysis because of your potency disturbances fifteen years ago, you would have been cured of that trouble and still have achieved your success in business."

"Aren't you contradicting yourself? If the driving power behind success-hunting is inner passivity, as you claim—the same passivity that caused my potency troubles—then by curing me, you would have made me at the same time a failure in business."

"That is a spurious conclusion. You forget that your business success in success-hunting could constitute a *normal* sublimation of passivity. The *neurotic* passivity, deposited in your potency disturbance, could have been eliminated and the remnants of passivity used productively in business."

"How do you differentiate between neurotic and sublimated passivity?"

"You will admit that a man who is impotent does not have public backing—he is, in fact, a slightly ridiculous figure. The successful businessman *has* public backing and admiration. Both your impotence and your business success are based on passivity warded off with activity—but one deposition is made under pressure of guilt and the other is not."

"I feel it's a trick—though I admit I don't see where the trick lies."

"There is no trick. Take clinical experience as a guide: every analyst can pride himself on the fact that *some* of his patients achieved great success in their specific fields *after* successful analysis. If your assumption were correct, that fact would be inexplicable. You're forgetting that every man fights a lifelong inner battle with passivity. The problem is one of *productive and unproductive self-damaging depositions in defense.*"

"I'm still skeptical. I believe it's safer to achieve success first and then analyze the 'remnants' of passivity. It's like the story of the man who went to Europe by ship in preference to taking a plane—in a plane, he said, 'You're a little *too* much in God's hands.'"

"How would you explain, then, the fact that men who previously were failures in business became remarkably successful after analysis?"

"I don't know. Anyhow, this is a pointless discussion, because if the patient weren't already a success he couldn't afford the analyst's fee."

"Your constant stressing of the fee shows your passivity: you feel overwhelmed and defend yourself by a persistent attack."

Third, we have: *Propelling impetus toward more and more success.* Inner tension, the outward manifestation of the success hunter's inner passivity, leads to a vicious circle. Instead of relaxing and enjoying the success he has achieved, the individual is driven demoniacally to reach for more and more. Experienced businessmen often deny that they are propelled by need of, or even desire for, more money: "I have all the money I need." Business success has become a game, and they continue the pursuit ostensibly to satisfy the "gaming instinct." Actually there is no instinct whatever involved; it is an inner guilt feeling that pushes them on so relentlessly. Pseudo aggression, materializing as achieved success, appeases the inner conscience only temporarily. After a time, the old reproach of inner passivity is renewed; hence a new alibi must be instigated. The unfortunate success hunter is on the move once more in his ceaseless search for the new—and short-lived—alibi.

The fourth characterization is: *Dissatisfaction and boredom if deprived of new business excitement and resulting opportunities to show off.* "Nothing is more difficult to endure than a series of pleasant days," a poet once said. This ironic complaint of Goethe's perfectly describes the plight of all those who cannot enjoy leisure, peace and quiet, of whom the success hunter is an outstanding example. Without excitement, life for him is not worth living.

The rationalizations brought forth to cover this pathological restlessness are manifold. The most typical is abundant energy: "I must have something with which to occupy my mind." Quite understandable, certainly; it is pleasanter to consider oneself a living dynamo than a perpetual alibi furnisher, and much more consoling to marvel at one's own inexhaustible energy than to admit to inner passivity necessitating inner refutation. Thus the merciful covering cloak of rationalization.

The typical dissatisfation and boredom experienced by the success hunter when new excitement is not provided arise from the inner passivity's temporarily not being covered by the current defense mechanism. This type of man often claims that he needs a challenge. The rationalization runs like this: "The easiest way to propel me into action is to say that something is impossible." What he cannot know is that his inner conscience immediately ·akes up the challenge with the reproachful goad: "If you weren't weakling you would find a solution." The resulting extraor- linary effort corresponds to one more passivity-disproving inner ılibi.

The success hunter is also fond of showing off before others, of presenting himself and his achievements for their envy and admiration. Everyone likes flattery to some degree, and the amount of hypocritical nonsense swallowed by even the ordinary man is remarkable. But there is a difference between being taken in by occasional flattery and depending constantly on the opinion of others. The greater the inner insecurity—basically, passivity—the greater will be that dependence. The success-hunter, because his inner passivity must have constant refutation from *outside* as well as inside, is dependent on a continuous diet of flattering approval: the quantity of such flattery thus substitutes for inner security.

Pangs of conscience are the genesis of the big businessman's brilliant ideas. He leads the list of psychic masochists of a "higher" order. I have found, with amazing regularity, that the deliberately thought-out decisions and ideas of this type of man came *after a period of depression and dissatisfaction, with relative lack of success.* On the other hand, successful intuition coincided with the moment in which torturing pangs of conscience were at a high point: thus the brilliant idea represented the desperate alibi.

It is interesting to observe that the superstition of the superior mental capacity of the big businessman is—just that, a superstition. Mental agility is demonstrated, certainly, in the situation described above, but the brilliant idea is not the result of any conscious or purely intellectual process. On the contrary, it is the result of last resources being mobilized under terrific pressure of guilt. The mental capacities of the big businessman might be compared to those of a prisoner hunting for a way of escape.

Paradoxical as it seems, one may say that if the big businessman is a good thinker, the characteristic will be displayed in his hobby life rather than in relation to his business success, of which it is not an integral part.

Fifth among the signs of the success hunter is: *Cynical outlook, hypersensitivity, and hypersuspiciousness.* "Every man has his price" is a cynical statement often made by the individual whose disregard for everything not connected with money leads him to make false conclusions about the rest of humanity. Cynicism is a complicated inner defense mechanism[1] denoting a never-ending battle with the inner conscience. The battle line is ambivalence: two contradictory feelings toward the same problem or person at the same time. When love and hate, admiration and contempt, or attachment and repulsion are felt simultaneously and with equal strength, the inner conscience objects, with the result that one is torn between contradictory feelings. One attempted way of resolving the painful indecision is to look for external allies as a means of proving to the inner conscience that everyone else harbors identical contradictory feelings. Every piece of cynicism, publicly uttered, is an unconscious invitation to the listener to admit that he feels as the cynic does. In attacking the venerated institutions and cherished beliefs of the outer world, the cynic unconsciously addresses a plea to the whole human race to give up its hypocrisy and admit that its feelings are the same as his.

In addition, by offending and provoking others with cynicism, the cynic satisfies his *warded-off* inner wish of passivity—for he is not only feared for the offensive statements but held in contempt as well. The neurotic cynic of course prefers to take the blame for the lesser crime and be abhorred for his pseudo aggression. The battle of alibis in neurotics is never ending.

The cynic is inwardly frightened, and the specific technique he uses is a form of whistling in the dark. This may be shown in still another way. The cynic is frequently hypersensitive, in direct contradiction to his professed aggressiveness. If everyone is, as he would like to believe, capable of every sort of dirty and underhanded trick, why be surprised if others act according to their principles? Were cynicism only a statement of facts concerning the darker side of humanity, it would automatically guarantee a protection from disappointments afflicted by the qualities complained of. That it is not is shown by the fact that the cynic, when

[1]"Psychology of Cynicism," *Psychoanalytische Bewegung*, 1933. In this study, sixty-four forms of cynicism are described. See Chapters I and II in the author's book *Talleyrand—Napoleon—Stendhal—Grabbe, Internationaler Psychoanalytischer Verlag*, 1935. See also Chapter IX ("Paradigms of Neurotic Antidotes for Feeling of Guilt: The Triad—Cynicism, Hypocrisy, Self-Derision") in *The Battle of the Conscience*, Washington Institute of Medicine, Washington, D. C., 1948.

he receives a disappointment, is deeply offended by the baseness and malice of the offender.

Especially vulnerable is the cynic confronted with human ingratitude. Why a man with—officially—so low an opinion of humankind should expect gratitude is something no cynic has ever explained. One might suppose, logically, that the cynic would react to ingratitude with a feeling of satisfaction at seeing one of his cherished tenets confirmed, but no; his reactions are always those of indignation and pessimism.

The mutually contradictory cynicism and hypersensitivity of the success hunter are further complicated by his habitual hyper-suspiciousness. Success does not make him secure, and he does not take the envy and enmity of his competitors with equanimity. He feels that people gang up on him; in other words, he becomes slightly paranoiacal.

Sixth, there is: *Contempt for and ruthlessness toward the unsuccessful.* Leniency toward the weak is unknown. A success hunter explained this peculiarly ruthless attitude in these words: "It's a tough game, and whoever goes into it must be prepared for it."

I asked why, and commented on his remarkably determined tone.

"That's the rule," he said. "Every game has its rules."

"Very well. I would like, however, to know the reasons."

"Business means making money."

"True enough. But is it necessary to cut your competitor's throat in order to make money?"

"No, only the sharks do that. But business is definitely not a humanitarian game."

This collection of tautologies was repeated endlessly by all the businessmen I questioned.

Alexandre Dumas the Younger said one hundred years ago: "Business? It's quite simple. It's other people's money."[2] How to maneuver that money into one's own pocket while still adhering to all the rules of the game (in order to avoid the district attorney and the grand jury) is the success hunter's problem. These banalities do not, of course, adequately explain the contempt of the

[2] *La Question d'Argent,* II, p. 7.

successful man for the man without money. Theoretically one might imagine that the successful individual would display reactions of pity, of superiority and pride, or a variety of feelings between. Contempt and ruthlessness are not understandable.

The reason for them seems to be a complicated psychic phenomenon, connected with our main thesis that the success hunter is at bottom a passive person. The unsuccessful man seems to provoke in him the inner reproach: "That is a mirror of yourself, you weakling." To counteract the reproach the defense of pseudo aggression is mobilized. Thus he strikes down the weakling, in projection.

Seventh, we have: *One-sided and opinionated I-know-better attitude in general.* The miracle of success elevates the successful man into a circle regarded by his naïve fellows as an elite group of the hyperclever, hyperknowledgeable and hypersmart. Both *external* esteem and *internal* victory (the individual having won the first round with his temporarily outsmarted inner conscience) push him into a position of ostensible omniscience. It is difficult to remain level-headed in such a situation, and the majority at once take upon themselves the roles of prophet and interpreter of events past, present, and future.

On the other hand, the man in his meteorlike rise feels the ambivalent approach of the environment. His vanity is increased by the knowledge that others admire him, but at the same time he is keenly aware of the doubters who attribute his success to pure luck and gloat over the possibility that it will not last. This skeptical attitude on the part of other people is doubly irritating just because it coincides with his own inner doubts. The typical resulting defense is obstinacy, the I-know-better attitude.

Eighth: *Hypochondriacal worries: doubts concerning continuous flow of ideas and luck.* Hypochondria is the success hunter's shadow. This is easily understandable, since it is the bodily expression of passivity. The specific choice of organ made by the individual has, of course, specific reasons behind it. The end effect, however, is always the same. The individual has a physical, rather than an intellectual, worry and the tormenting organ is an unconsciously self-appointed dictator, the victim a self-appointed serf.

The success hunter's difficulties are increased by his fidelity to the prescribed he-man attitude of stoicism. Unless he has had the luck, psychosomatically speaking, to choose a currently socially correct symptom, he hasn't even the right to complain in public but must keep his troubles to himself, thus increasing the load of worry. Even if the nature of his symptom gives him the right to come into the open with his complaints, he must exercise caution; otherwise his enemies may begin to look forward to his funeral.

Parallel with tension, hypochondria, and worry goes another set of inner tortures—doubts concerning the continuation of his ideas and luck. Something keeps telling him that his luck is running out. Even his most malicious enemy, while audibly crediting his success to luck, really believes that some personal initiative was involved. The success hunter himself is inwardly more skeptical; his constant fear of the sudden collapse of his success shows that he has no confidence in his ability to sustain it. These doubts concerning the stability and continuation of success prove conclusively that his inner conscience is on the warpath. As a patient put it: "I have convinced the world that my success represents real merit—but not myself." The tragedy of the success hunter, with his never-ending need of putting up a front, is that he lives beyond his emotional means.

Ninth: *Inability to enjoy the simple pleasures of life.* The success hunter has no real friends. This observation has been confirmed time and again. As soon as one reaches a really high income bracket he is confronted by envy, parasitism, enmity; and though he may mingle with a restricted group of people on the same social and economic level, the success hunter is usually lonely. He has acquaintances, but no friends. The reason is complicated, but basically it is reducible to the fact that he does not need friends. He needs admirers, people who will satisfy his craving for flattery. These serve the purpose of strengthening his inner defenses by perpetually attesting to his greatness. Real friends are not a source of hypocritical flattery, nor are they full of ingratiating humility; therefore the success hunter does without them.

Friendship being out of the question, there remains the possibility of a normal, tender relationship with a woman—but the success hunter is also incapable of this. The inner passivity that may push him into marriage with a shrew, or cause him to surround himself with parasitic girl friends, prevents his taking the normal course.

What money can buy, he buys. Unfortunately for him, love and the enjoyment of simple pleasures are not purchasable. The success hunter of course goes through the motions. His car is the most expensive, his country estate the most elaborate; everything he owns is of the best quality financially obtainable. But that thin satisfaction wears off very quickly, emptiness remains. He may be afflicted, too, with a money neurosis, department miser, in which case every dollar he spends causes him further torture.

Tenth: *Hidden depression, warded off with tempered megalomania and extensive air of importance.* The typical success hunter presents an outward picture of confidence and self-assurance. Penetrate the veneer, however, and you find a massive neurotic depression. One may safely state that the predominant mood of this type of person is extensive depression. The typical defensive cover is overoptimism bordering on slight megalomania, combined with a pompous air of importance.

To give an example, I was consulted by a New York businessman, one of the most successful in his field, who complained of constant tension and worry over his ability to finish the amount of work he daily prescribed for himself. This self-enforced overcrowded schedule entailed not only extensive business dealings but also working for a number of cultural and humanitarian institutions. "I worry day and night," he said. "For years I've managed to do every bit of the work I set myself, but that knowledge doesn't help. I know I could curtail my killing schedule—I promise myself constantly to work less—but I can't seem to do it. I just keep on overworking—and worrying about it. It's fantastic."

I explained that he lived beyond his emotional means. This suggestion was accepted immediately but countered with the argument that if analysis were to change his neurotic tension he couldn't work at all.

The man's story was supplemented, by his wife, with several details which he had left out; e.g., symptoms of impotence, pathological stinginess, and irrational rage. However, he decided not to enter treatment—because he could not afford the fee.

Happy people, a rare species anywhere, are not to be found even among success hunters. More inner misery obtains there than in any other group of money neurosis.

*Eighty-three years! I cannot decide whether I am
content in remembering these many years and how I
spent them. How much useless business! Unre-
warded attempts, boring routine, exaggerated emotions, spent energy, wasted abilities, loss of mental
balance, destroyed illusions, worn-out attachments!
And the end? Moral and physical exhaustion, complete discouragement and deep distaste for the
past . . .*

TALLEYRAND'S *Mémoires*

5. THE FORMULA FOR SUCCESS,
OR SELF-SCRUTINY AND WHAT PRICE SUCCESS?

The success hunter in the guise of big businessman
is generally admired for his quick grasp of an advantage, his energy and his mysterious affinity for
luck. He is the fairy-tale hero in modern dress.

Examined psychiatrically, the story of success
looks somewhat different. To begin with, success
does not commence at the moment of the brilliant
idea. Its foundations were laid in childhood, before
the fifth year, when the end result of the infantile
conflict was definitely established. This end result,
in the specific case of the success hunter, is one of

great inner passivity counteracted by great inner reproach occasioned by precisely that passivity.

Inner passivity plus inner reproach spells double inner conflict. The lifelong struggle with this double conflict forces the success hunter to take defensive measures: he will establish, unconsciously, a strong alibi to disprove the inner accusation. The alibi—aggression of the compensatory variety—in future will cause people to admire his energy, iron will, and consistency.

The psychic structure of the successful man differs in no way from that of the timid failure; the two struggle with an identical conflict. The difference between them is that the former *masters the defensive aggression, and the latter cannot.*

An anecdote is told about one of Napoleon's generals, a man undistinguished for intelligence, who once, out of dire necessity, came up with a really brilliant idea. Napoleon was holding, during one of his great campaigns, an important council of war, and for hours no one had been allowed to leave the council room for any purpose. The hitherto rather dull general, who suffered from prostate trouble and was in urgent need of relieving himself, finally could bear it no longer—and in this dangerously pressing situation suddenly presented to Napoleon a brilliant strategic idea, thus ending the council. Napoleon was thoroughly baffled. "And I always considered him an idiot!" he remarked to his adjutant.

Substitute for the general's prostate pressure the pressure of conscience because of inner passivity and you have the genesis of the brilliant ideas in the success hunter. A not very romantic simile, but a true one. With amazing regularity, I found that the real and decisive conception of *the* great venture, the great thought or plan in this type came after *a long spell of depression and dissatisfaction with relative lack of success. The "intuition" coincided with that moment when pangs of torturing conscience were at the high point.* The brilliant idea represented the desperate alibi.

It is interesting to observe that there is a general misconception about big businessmen of the success-hunting variety. Their superior mental capacity is greatly overrated. True, quickness was there when the brilliant idea was conceived, but the point here is that it was neither a conscious nor purely intellectual process. Quite the contrary: under the *terrific inner pressure of guilt* the last resources were mobilized, as in the case of the Napoleonic general.

The mental capacities of the success hunters I observed were those of a prisoner looking for escape. Stendhal remarked in *La Chartreuse de Parme* that the prisoner is superior to the jailer in one respect: he thinks in a more concentrated fashion about escape than the jailer, who feels secure about preventing escape.

What of the follow-through process in business? In this process the superior intelligence is not discernible; it is, for the most part, a banal process, following specific long-established paths. Only outsiders take this banal part of the venture as a miracle. Even the business people, the serious insiders, don't brag about it.

In discussing this problem with a patient at one time, he was impatient with all I had to say and kept pressing me for what he called a formula for success. As his analysis was brought almost to a standstill by his resistance-based insistence, I finally acceded. The formula looked even more impressive when placed upon paper in simulated mathematical form:

$$S = \frac{IP + FPAD(MA + C) + V}{M + FEC}$$

IP stands for inner passivity.
FPAD for frantic pseudo-aggressive defense mechanism, leading to mental agility (MA) and consistency (C).
V denotes unimpaired imagination or vision.[1]
M denotes market.
FEC, favoring external circumstances.

For success of the success-hunter type one needs a specific psychic constitution, *acquired unconsciously* in childhood. In other

[1]Genetically, the qualities of imagination and "vision" have humble origins, connected with voyeurism (Peeping). If there is neurotic inhibition of voyeurism, lack of imagination results—with, in the case of artistic people, damaging effects in later life. See the author's book *The Writer and Psychoanalysis*, Brunner's Psychiatric Books, N. Y., 1954 (second, enlarged edition).

words, this psychic constitution is not inborn and cannot be attained by following good advice: *it is a specific neurotic sickness with its own unconsciously self-produced self-cure.* Acquired as an end result of one's infantile conflict, it may be used either productively or unproductively, depending again on unconscious factors. Therefore, the first prerequisite for success is beyond conscious control, and success itself may be the result of a productive sickness. The successful man of that variety, it can now be seen, is not the strong man of legend, the fairy-tale hero, but the possessor of a productive compensatory alibi for inner passivity. It should be stressed once more *that normal businessman and neurotic success hunter are by no means identical.*

The passivity of the success hunter is clearly visible in his sex life. Typically his marriage is based on submission to a shrew, an aggressive woman who exploits him financially and holds him in complete dominance. Submitting weakly, he nevertheless feels abused and flees from domestic difficulties into business problems.

His wife's hold on him is based on two factors: inner passivity and poor potency coupled with sexual insecurity. These facts usually are totally unsuspected by the outer world, which innocently assumes that the strong man of business must also be a strong man at home. Actually, normal sex life is, among big businessmen of the success-hunting variety, rather the exception than the rule. Though not every success hunter suffers from a potency disturbance, many of them have one or more personality difficulties.

For example, a man may marry, on the alibi principle, a nice, kind woman—only to find himself impotent with her and attracted to other, more aggressive women. Thus he gets his daily dose of injustice in extramarital affairs. Or he may be impotent with his wife but take an aggressive "wolf"-attitude toward other women. Priding himself on his conquests, he conveniently overlooks the fact that he conquers because he pays.

Sometimes he remains unmarried, giving the impression of enjoying a full sex life as a bachelor. In a number of cases women patients with leanings toward prostitution have reported that, after being invited to the apartment of such unmarried industrial magnates of the success-hunting variety, they were treated to an expensive meal, a good deal of conversation—and nothing else. These women were used for the purpose of disguising impotence and bolstering before the public a legend of sexual prowess.

Unimpaired potency under neurotic conditions (e.g., the situation of the forbidden, an infantile remnant accounting for impotence in legalized marriage) cannot be called normal. It is especially grotesque and rather tragicomic to witness a situation in which (as often happens) the man who is impotent in marriage but a great lover extramaritally, permits his masochistic psychic tendencies to find expression in jealousy of the paid girl friend.

Neurotic admixtures exist in every human being. Everyone harbors within him an unconscious part of the personality which is unfriendly to himself. The question of whether or not the individual needs psychoanalysis depends on how great his unconscious difficulties are, and—even more important—how well he is equipped to cope with these difficulties. Advice to enter treatment is justified only in those cases in which the neurotic admixtures have become quantitatively increased to a degree where they cause the individual serious trouble in his professional and emotional life.

To apply these general statements to the specific problem of success and failure: I do not believe that everyone who hasn't achieved spectacular success should enter upon psychiatric-psychoanalytical treatment. Nor do I believe, needless to say, that every cured analytic patient automatically becomes a genius with the ability to achieve every conscious aim, including the acquisition of a million dollars. I believe simply that successful treatment brings the patient to that point—and only that point—which he would have reached himself *if he had not been neurotic.*

In other words, analytical treatment, if successful, gives the patient access to his highest potentialities. Failure in business venture is not necessarily a signal that treatment is needed. First *should come a period of self-scrutiny* to determine whether there exists a pattern of repetitive mistakes. Only if this self-scrutiny reveals to the individual an inkling of such a neurotic pattern, a pattern which cannot be corrected by himself, should psychiatric aid be sought.

The elimination of cases susceptible of self-correction is necessary for another and very practical reason: there are not enough psychiatrists to take care of all neurotics. At this writing there are only five thousand in the entire country, half of them entirely occupied with institutional work.

In making the recommended self-scrutiny, the following ten points will be helpful.

1. Take stock of your abilities. Marked discrepancy between proven gifts and achievements indicates that failure may be of neurotic origin.

2. Evaluate the mistakes made in a specific venture, checking to determine whether inexperience, wrong timing, the weakness of the original idea, lack of ordinary foresight or your psychic make-up is to blame.

3. Take into account a cross section of your achievements. If there is a predominance of failure on decisive points, the situation is suspicious.

4. Don't overlook the usual success-failure ratio. One successful idea out of ten is the average.

5. Look for repetitiveness. If you always quarrel with your partner, always get in trouble with your customers, always use wrong timing, and keep coming up against the same stumbling block, neurosis is indicated.

6. Watch for the habit of making excuses for your failures (such as blaming the meanness of others; on the other hand unawareness of the possibility of encountering such meanness can only be accounted for by neurotic pseudo naïveté).

7. Clarify your faulty psychological evaluation of your antagonists. Remember: psychic masochists have a peculiar approach to reality: they are hypersubmissive confronted with aggressive people, and cruel toward the weaker. A confusing fact for the layman to accept is that, by unconsciously provoking the stronger person, psychic masochists cash in on their wish to be kicked around. These two techniques differ only phenomenologically; the inner aim and result are identical.

8. Scrutinize the standard excuse: "How was I to know?" Look back and try to determine whether you overlooked, in any given situation, clearly indicative signs of the outcome.

9. Estimate the amount of emotional involvement after failure: to dwell upon fantasies of being unjustly treated and to waste time in unproductive revenge ideas is plainly neurotic.

10. Watch your psychic reactions after failure. If psychic energy sags downward for a longer time than usual, if depression persists and your tendency is to retire into resignation,[2] neurosis is present. Normally no one accepts the fact of failure; narcissism and self-esteem continue to be propelling factors even after defeat.

The success hunter has three ambitions: to make millions, to become famous—and then to live happily ever after. The chances of his achieving the first two are rather slim, but—assuming that he does—he has even less chance of achieving the third. Success breeds worry and unhappiness; the fruits of success are, contrary to popular belief, far from sweet. It is the exceptional man indeed who makes a fortune and retires to enjoy life, whatever that may mean for him. Success for most men means increased work as well as worry. If the success hunter who has achieved his ambition should take an honest look backward, he would find that success has acted as a sponge to absorb his vital energies. The fruits of his labors are enjoyed not by himself but by the parasites, inside and outside his family, who are his beneficiaries.

Two consolations are left to him: first, his narcissistic-exhibitionistic pleasure, and second, the satisfaction of having refuted (if only temporarily) the reproach of his inner conscience pertaining to passivity.

Here it must be said once more that no one begins the nerve-

[2]Especially if you are "crushed" by the hindsight prophets: *Of all the horrid, hideous notes of woe, / Sadder than owl-songs of the midnight blasts / Is the portentous phrase "I told you so."* BYRON, *Don Juan*

racking climb to success because he decided to do so. Faust's: "You believe you impel, and are yourself impelled" is applicable. The *vis a tergo* is the conflict of passivity plus the necessity of furnishing an unconscious alibi.

Happiness and the exaggerated search for success are frequently incompatible. The inner guilt that was the original impelling force is insatiable. Success means short-lived elation followed inevitably by worry, tension, and uncertainty; nothing is ever enough; there must always be more and more money, fame, power. If the success hunter's reasoning powers tell him that he ought to be satisfied with what he has achieved, he becomes bored. He rationalizes that his abundant energy needs an outlet. This explains why some businessmen lose interest when the success of a venture becomes assured. They look frantically for new ventures, new outlets, sometimes to settle for hypochondria, latent depression or aggravation of an organic disease. This type of inner passivity is so great that the success hunter cannot even die peacefully. He cannot accept illness with the stoicism and resignation of the average person; even on his deathbed he is tortured by the inner reproach that if he were not a weakling this couldn't happen to him.

This rather gloomy picture does not mean that one should shun success; it must be remembered that *there is no voluntary decision involved in the making of a success hunter.* The average person possesses neither the psychic constitution nor the resulting self-cure necessary for spectacular success. What is important for him is to accept his limitations (in reality, lack of a specific neurotic disease) without bitterness or self-accusation.

To envy the success hunter and the "miracle" of success is to overlook the fact that for the normal person *inner contentment* is the important thing, the *real* thing.[3]

[3]As, conversely, psychic masochism is the "real thing" for neurotics—though they are not, of course, aware of it consciously.

PART THREE: THE GAMBLER

Why did my father's advice to use the three Rs—re-morse, regret, repentance—not help me to overcome my gambling?

Question asked by a patient, a gambler,
when in a losing period

6. THE GAMBLER, SINGLEHANDED AGAINST THE WHOLE WORLD

The gambler[1] is the classical example of the individual burdened with money neurosis who—as opposed to others of the same species but with differing specificities—never succeeds. He is defeated before he starts, though he does not know that, or would not believe it if he did. In fact, no other neurotic is so thoroughly or so consistently hopeful of one day

[1]By "gambler" is not meant the bookmaker, the gambling-house proprietor or any others engaged in the operation of games of chance for profit. Meaning of the word as used here is: "one who habitually stakes or risks something on an uncertain event."

winning a fortune. Informed that gambling is a neurotic disease requiring psychiatric treatment, he replies with full conviction that he has no need of psychiatry—all he needs is more working capital to tide him over his present temporary losing streak. . . .

The gambler is fanatically optimistic in his conviction that he and the million to which he aspires are only a few inches apart. "Just give me time and a little money," he says confidently, "and I'll make it."

Gambling represents the prime example of misusing money for the solution of inner conflicts completely unrelated to money. The gambler's career does not start at the race track or gambling table, or in the broker's office; it starts in the nursery, and the cause of the trouble is once more the triad of undigested conflicts: infantile megalomania, aggression, and masochistic elaboration of both.

It is virtually impossible to convince an inveterate gambler that he cannot win. His argument is always the same: since money changes hands in gambling, why should it not flow into his hands? And what about people who actually *have* won large amounts of money? he asks triumphantly.

It is true that money changes hands in gambling, and that a gambler sometimes wins: what is missing from the gambler's deduction is the fact that the winning of money is only his conscious, official aim in gambling. If he actually treated gambling as a practical way of making money, he would quit when he had won. Instead, what happens? The gambler, having received the badly needed confirmation that winning is possible, continues to gamble until he has lost everything once more.

Here is an experience related by a patient. While visiting a fashionable French gambling resort, and after having gone several times to the casino, he paid a social call on the manager of that establishment, to whom he had a letter of introduction. After an exchange of amenities the manager asked whether he had visited the casino. "Of course," was the answer. "I have even won a few thousand francs." At this the manager earnestly advised him to leave town at once: "If you don't, you will continue to gamble until you've lost everything. *We make money because the gambler can't stop when he loses, and especially when he wins!*"

This is the crux of the myth of winning at gambling. It is a myth because the inner structure of the gambling addict carries its own losing bacillus. Were the gambler a rational person, he would not, first of all, choose a profession so filled with uncertainties; and second, he would understand that occasional winning is not a promise of further winnings, but a warning sign to take his leave. What happens, however, is that luck smiles once and the gambler mistakes that rare mimetic expression for a promise of permanency. In the end he is bitterly disillusioned; a man may become rich by gambling, but he will not die a rich man. The typical gambler—if he escapes suicide—dies penniless. Why? Because he cannot stop gambling until he has lost literally everything.

The reason for this is simple once it is understood. Psychiatric-psychoanalytic experience proves that *the gambler's unconscious aim is to lose.*[2]

[2]This theory was first propounded by me in "Psychology of the Gambler," *Imago*, 1936; later in "The Gambler—a Misunderstood Neurotic," *Journal of Criminal Psychopathology*, IV, 3, 379-93, 1943; Chapter VI, #15, pp. 254—65 in *The Basic Neurosis*; A summing-up may be found in my book, *The Psychology of Gambling* (Hill & Wang, New York, 1957).

In five minutes I accumulated 400 gold pieces at roulette. I should have left at that moment, but a strange feeling came over me to challenge Fate. It was the wish to give Fate a punch in the nose and show her my tongue.

DOSTOEVSKI, The Gambler

7. THE GAMBLER'S UNCONSCIOUS AIM—TO LOSE

The moment the gambler has played his stake, the outcome of the game is beyond his control. This is the simple *objective* fact. *Subjectively* the gambler feels that he can control the outcome: he hopes to influence it by wishing, and behaves as if it were possible for certain acts of his own to bring about the desired result—as witness the gambler's numerous superstitions. He uses a shabby, torn wallet because once, when it was new, he won while carrying it; or he avoids certain dates and numbers because they are unlucky for him. He will abstain from, or perform, certain magic little actions because he knows from experience that they carry specific meaning. Sometimes the more intelligent gambler will laugh at his superstitions—though he continues to obey them. A patient once admitted that while watching on television a certain race upon which he had placed a bet, he kept crossing and recrossing his legs in a certain way—meaningful actions performed for the purpose of influencing the jockey.

Behind this admission lies the whole extent of the gambler's infantile megalomania. Infantile megalomania came into conflict with the reality principles as communicated by mother and, later, father. The resultant fury of the child was either handled or neurotically *mishandled* by the child; in the latter case the aggression was turned, because of guilt, against the child himself, and secondarily "libidinized," a process leading invariably to psychic masochism, *the happiness-in-unhappiness pattern.*

Hence an adult promoting infantile megalomania in a decisive life situation automatically puts in operation the masochistic elaboration. This is the self-imposed penalty for unrelinquished infant pleasures, only secondarily *made pleasurable.*

The repeated fate of the psychic masochist is to provoke, unconsciously, a stronger power (representing the giant of the nursery, Mother). If this is done with ingenuity, a refusal follows, and this *inwardly self-approved* refusal is mistaken by the neurotic for a refusal from *outside;* in other words, he sees himself as the innocent victim of outside malice. Against such malice he now fights his battle of alibis with all the pseudo aggression at his disposal. It looks like a case of justified self-defense; what it represents actually is a desperate inner alibi: "I don't want to be *refused;* I want to *get.*" Since only kicks, refusals, and defeats are forthcoming, the self-deceiving innocent-guilty "victim" may glory in his masochistic martyrdom.

The gambler unconsciously deludes himself twice: first, consciously, in believing that he wants to win money (*the battle of dollars*); and second, in unconsciously believing that he is acting aggressively against the educational commands which aimed to destroy his stubborn infant belief that he could do whatever he pleased—the substratum of infantile megalomania (*the battle of alibis*). Unknowingly the gambler is still, as an adult, fighting the educational rules with pseudo-aggressive weapons. Inwardly he delivers a soliloquy, directed at his upbringers, which might be phrased somewhat as follows: "All your talk about normal conduct was pretty hypocritical, wasn't it? Look around you. 'Work leads to success'? 'Logic and consistency are reliable guideposts'? Well, at the gambling table, at the race track, and on the stock exchange millions of dollars change hands every day—and people get rich without work. *Chance* is the important thing. I've got no use for all your ridiculous normal rules of conduct!"

It is exactly this rebellion against educational commands which made Dostoevski intuitively put into the mouth of his gambler the words: "It was the wish to give Fate a punch in the nose and show her my tongue." The gesture and the language used to express it are relics of the nursery—where the trouble started.

Having unconsciously provided himself with the necessary excuses, the gambler proceeds to his *real* wish: to be masochistically refused. This wish is unconscious; under no conditions could it occur consciously to the gambler himself.

The real and dynamically decisive factor in gambling—the happiness-in-unhappiness pattern—manifests itself twice in the course of gambling. First, it provides the mysterious thrill in gambling, which, as honest gamblers admit, is even more exciting than the hope of winning. That thrill is, according to the same honest gamblers, difficult to describe. One patient described it as *"pleasurable-painful tension."* I subsequently submitted this formulation to a series of patients who were addicts of gambling and found that most of them confirmed its accuracy. It was interesting to observe, in this connection, the mixture of surprise and hesitation with which these patients reacted to being asked to check on their feelings. Though all of them were familiar with the thrill in question, none had ever attempted to define it, and some acted as though there was some sort of sacrilege involved in even discussing it. "Let sleeping dogs lie," said one. "But they are not sleeping at all," was my reply. "In your case they are very much awake."

The reason for this reluctance is plain: understanding of the thrill robs it of mystery to the masochistic substructure, hence is to be avoided at all costs. One patient finally answered, under pressure, that the nearest he could come was to make a comparison with a particular situation remembered from elementary school days: he had come home with a poor report card, to find his mother out, and had waited an hour for her to return. "That hour of waiting, knowing I was going to receive the usual spanking, produced in me a feeling of terror—and some kind of elation."

This recollection contains an elaboration of the "elation in terror" experienced in the gambler's thrill. The elation corresponds in more superficial, though also unconscious, layers to the lesser crime of pseudo aggression: the gambler oversteps educational commands. It is shifted to that point as an admission of the *lesser* crime, though genetically it belongs to the *real* crime of masochistic pleasure.

The case of the gambler may be stated as follows: having become "stabilized on the rejection level" as the end result of his specific infantile conflict, he re-enacts in his gambling the whole rigmarole of his wishes and defense. The unconscious wish, "I want to be refused," is counteracted by severe inner guilt. To assuage the latter, the mechanical gambling device and its animate substitutes become unconsciously identified with the infantile prototypes. These must, by their unjust and refusing behavior, feed the alibi: "I am just the innocent victim." Losses provide the necessary proof of the alibi.

Hence my conviction that the gambler—unconsciously—wants to lose. In the long run he always loses.

To formulate it another way: the gambler risks good money for the bogus coin of his inner wishes and defenses. Since no exchange rate exists between inner and outer reality, he takes monetary losses as part payment for his happiness-in-unhappiness.

These losses, and the depression which follows, provide the second "masochistic installment" mentioned above. The depression has a complicated defensive structure. It seemingly pertains to mourning over being unloved (originally, by the first upbringer). In inner reality the despair and depression are a form of appeasement: "conscience money" paid for the proof that the gambler does not enjoy his psychic masochism—as the inner indictment justifiably claims he does. Being a psychic masochist, he cannot lose—at least intrapsychically—by misusing his depression secondarily, as well, for the purpose of extracting masochistic pleasure. In fact, in this way he adds to his masochistic bank account. The unavoidable consequence is that his *actual* bank account dwindles.

Hence the three Rs (remorse, regret, repentance), reported by the gambler patient as his father's recommended remedy, are out of necessity ineffective. They can only add fuel to the battle of alibis and secondary masochistic pleasure.

No less unfortunate is the fact that the shocked and sympathetic outsider, who wants to help, is prevented from doing so by two things: first, obviously, by the lack of treatment facilities, and second, by the gambler's psychology (tomorrow I will win). I quote from a letter written by a lady living in a western state:

Dear Sir:

My interest in a bright likable student who is addicted to gambling has led me to search in libraries for information which might be helpful. Your article "The Gambler—a Misunderstood Neurotic" contains practically the only encouraging words I've found. What you say is true.

It has been my problem and opportunity to study a most tragic case for a period of twenty months. It was agitated and developed by army life. The victim is a young man about twenty-four years of age who sees all the evils connected with the game, and knows where he is going to end up, but can not quit. He is scared of the future and well may he be. He has tried desperately hard to quit and I know he has done his best. We have had some agonizing sessions. He does not confide in me for sympathy but talks through sheer desperation. He does not want to live in the gutter, as he calls it. For six years he has struggled and tried to quit; the last three years he has become almost panic-stricken, which does not help, I reckon, in this case. While he gambles he loves it because he can think of nothing else. Then he hates it because of what it does to him. But when he gets money he can hardly wait until he gets down there. I have known him to work several weeks very hard, and turn it all over to the boys. He is ashamed of his lack of will power.

Yes, he does resent authority but is sweet and pliable as a child if reasoned with at the right time and led instead of or-dered. This is definitely a left-over from childhood, other issues entering in the picture: a good stepmother, in her way, and an extremely stern father who explained nothing and did not rea-son. What I have learned about the case is from various sources and coincidental but authentic. The father has spent many hours gambling for years (small gambling, I think) but has will power enough not to undermine his business or job.

According to the Veterans' Administration the boy is physi-cally unable to hold a job long. The boy is very much interested in going to college, likes physics and electricity, but can not keep away from the gambling joint. At present he can not concentrate for long at a time, perhaps on account of the game, perhaps on account of nervous trouble. He can study spasmodically but can not make a regular schedule. He is constantly saying that he must get himself in order so that he can hold himself to schedule. He is fighting himself and I would say against nerve exhaustion.

He is so tired except when under nerve tension, and gambling means nerve tension. He is happier when he has spent his money. I believe he unconsciously wants to lose, as you claim, but he has the gambler's philosophy—"Tomorrow I will win," or "Today is my day." Without doubt he has the gambler's disease. It is an obsession with him. He is a victim of circumstance: growing up under almost complete misunderstanding, ignorant concern-ing life in general, sweet and good as a boy but lacking the proper foundation to take the knocks of life. Being sensitive, he then became hard—or tried to, and became bitter.

Apparently the only change which I have been able to accom-plish is that he is less bitter, especially toward his father. He finally said to me "If my father did the best he knew how, my hat is off to him." That was something for him to say. He wears a gay mask, but few know what a desperate struggle is going on. One of his college instructors knows and is concerned, but can do nothing it seems.

He is a wonderful fellow, worth saving. He cannot hold out a great while longer. You know the outcome: suicide or the penitentiary. Can you help? I am willing to pay some, and might be able to get some from the Veterans' Administration.

The conception, "The gambler unconsciously wants to lose," is so difficult to accept that even when a tangential approach is employed, the distasteful problem is shifted and attenuated. Paradigmatic is a recent Hollywood movie called *The Lady Gambles.* The psychological substructure of the gambling lady is reduced to guilt for having "killed" her mother in the process of being born. Obviously it is senseless to blame a newborn child for matricide—therefore, to get around that absurdity, the thesis is put forward that an unconsciously half-homosexual older sister instilled the guilt in the child. In other words, the aggression and guilt connected with it—even a half admission of Lesbianism— are preferred to the dreary fact of psychic masochism. Ironically, this pseudo-psychological picture was rejected, in a review given it by a leading weekly, as too "Freudian."

Another absurdity encountered in literature is the perennial application of love as a cure for gambling. Though love has many virtues, unfortunately it has no efficacy as a remedy for the gambling habit.

I experience the same strange tension in business and gambling.

A big businessman of the success-hunter variety

8. ARE GAMBLING AND BUSINESS IDENTICAL?

In general, nobody admits to being a gambler. The negative moral connotations attached to gambling result in rather indignant protests even from the people who are caught, let us say, with their cards down.

I have frequently encountered people who frankly admitted to gambling addiction. The situation in which the admission took place, however, was exceptional: the specific situation of resistance (during the course of psychoanalytic treatment) after being shown deep repressed passivity, masochistically tinged. These particular gamblers were success hunters.

Mr. X., after having been proven, as he expressed it, guilty of passivity, was deeply disturbed. He argued the point, first morally, then intellectually, finally appealing to my better feelings. Being a psychic masochist, he argued pseudo cleverly, leaving himself open to contradiction. Inwardly he knew that he was building up, and defending, a losing bastion. This went on for some time; then one day he said: "Well, Doctor, I've taken stock of the situation, and I've decided that in order to convince you that in my case you're wrong in your assumption of masochistic passivity—especially as a propelling factor in business—I'll have to tell you something I've never admitted to you before."

"Before you divulge this secret," I said, "there's one point I'd like clarified: why are you so desperately anxious to convince me?"

"Isn't that necessary?"

"Not at all. You consulted me because of your marital troubles, including impotence. We analyzed that difficulty successfully; you regained your potency. In the course of treatment it became apparent that your domestic troubles were only a part of your neurosis—your hyperexcitement, your constant tension in business plainly being different manifestations of the same trouble. I asked you whether you wanted to change in that respect as well, and you agreed quite enthusiastically that you did, since you understood perfectly the lifelong advantages for the prolongation of your life. We made good progress in that respect too. Now you rebel—seemingly at a tangential problem: the reason for your interest in business. Don't you see that the wish to convince me can only be an expression of your guilty conscience?"

"How so?"

"Why don't you simply say to yourself 'The man is obviously wrong on that point. So what? I got what I wanted from the treatment—more than I expected, even. That's enough. To hell with his opinion.' "

"I don't know—I just feel that I *have* to convince you. May I tell you my secret?"

"Go ahead."

"Well, I'm an occasional gambler. You remember you asked me about gambling. I denied that I gambled—though you seemed not to believe me. I didn't tell you the whole truth then, but now I'm less inhibited."

"If I understand you correctly, you were withholding important material—which you submit now because it may bolster your alibi?"

"Yes."

"Is this what you want to say? 'I am not driven into my business tension, as you believe, by an *inner defense against passivity*, but by a *gambling instinct?*'"

"Correct."

"You mean I formulated correctly what you wanted to say? Objectively, the statement is incorrect—it does not correspond to the facts."

"I suppose now you're going to demolish my good honest confession!"

"Yes, because what you've confessed to is simply the *lesser* crime! Since many people gamble, gambling seems to you consciously less objectionable than inner masochistic passivity, which in fact—consciously—offends your ideas of what constitutes a he-man. The situation is similar to one we went through in an earlier stage of your analysis when, confronted with your self-damaging tendencies and their irrationality, you were asked whether you understood your psychic masochism or preferred being thought a moron. You chose to plead guilty to being, in some situations, a moron."

"That's a malicious interpretation!"

"When you use the word interpretation your intonation is that of a lady exclaiming in disgust over a four-letter word. May I remind you that this same frowned-upon interpretation (combined with emotional repetitions in the transference) restored your potency?"

"I can't explain my feelings—I can only register them. And I tell you truthfully that my tension in business and my tension when gambling are identical."

"That's a correct observation, but you don't understand the *productive* and *unproductive* depositions of those same feelings."

"O.K., so I'm at fault. Could you give me in a few words the psychology of gambling?"

"The tension in gambling corresponds to the masochist's wish to prove that mother (father) is unjust and refusing. This infantile and repressed situation is shifted to the gambling machine, horses, stocks, cards, and the gambling opponent. *Unconsciously the gambler wants to lose:* only by losing can he prove how unjust and refusing the infantile images are. But—and that 'but' is important—in the more superficial (hence defensive though also unconscious) layers, the gambler uses pseudo aggression toward the educational authorities of the nursery. He scoffs ironically at all the pedagogic rules aimed at teaching the child that logic, consistency, and hard work are steppingstones to correct behavior and success.

"Gambling is but one more manifestation of the mechanism of the self-provoked failure triad: 'I unconsciously provoke refusal; I see only that other people are unkind and refusing, and I fight them; I pity myself and cry in the corner over poor little me!' The additional, and specific, factor in gambling is the narcissistic masochistic defensive necessity of constant rebellion against the educational ABCs."

"Fine, specious, and, as usual, pseudo-cleverly concocted! That's the danger of analytical interpretations: they don't make sense, they just make *pseudo*-sense—and a hoax is put over on me."

"That's your real resistance talking, not your pseudo resistance. Your statement reminds me of a laudatory criticism of one of my books that appeared in a Michigan newspaper: "The author combines Freudian theory with a very reasonable understanding of human nature." The juxtaposition amused me; the critic's statement was, however, in contradiction to yours, meant as a compliment."

"But even if your, quote, interpretation, unquote, is correct, it applies only to gamblers who lose. You cannot deny that gamblers do sometimes win."

"Unconsciously the gambler wants to lose—that wish is just a later manifestation of his wish to nullify his mother as a 'giving' person. *Only by losing can he prove her refusing attitude.* The guilt, penance, and "conscience money" are shifted intrapsychically to the alleged aggression, released via an attack on parental authority, which, of course, does not approve of the irrationality of gambling. Both sources contribute to the wish to lose. Your argument that gamblers sometimes win is spurious. True, they have winning streaks—but in the long run *every* gambler loses."

"How do you explain the tension in gambling?"

"It's the same situation as that of the child who, by provoking the teacher and giving the wrong answer deliberately, gets a bad mark and comes home with the bad report, expecting a sound thrashing. The fearful expectation of a thrashing, masochistically tinged, corresponds to the gambler's tension."

"Where does the elation of occasionally winning come in? Isn't that a contradiction? If the gambler wants to lose, the elation should come with losing, not winning."

"Now you're being naïve—confusing consciousness and unconsciousness. Remember that the human being lives with, and by, his inner defenses. The inner defense of the masochist is pseudo aggression; hence, when the gambler wins, his defense seems to be confirmed: he has put one over on his accusing conscience, and feels elated. When he loses, he has got what he unconsciously wanted, but must ward off the reproachful conscience, hitting out at that pleasure—hence his covering depression as an alibi."

"Aren't you overlooking one little detail? *Real*—not imaginary —money is involved in gambling too."

"The infantile game is shifted to reality values. The money of the nursery is composed of love, punishment, and masochistic elaboration of both."

"It certainly seems pretty foolish to gamble in order to *lose*."

"It's also pretty silly to believe that gambling can be a method of earning money."

"Well, let me think it over."

At the next appointment the patient appeared refreshed and

reassured—not, as soon became apparent, because he had digested the discussed theory, but because he had found a new argument. He began triumphantly:

"What you told me yesterday just strengthens my argument. If the masochistic tension in gambling is the thing the gambler is after, then my excitement in business is caused by the very same gaming spirit!"

"You remind me of a man accused of parking his car in a restricted area who defends himself by saying that at the time the car was parked, *he* was raping a minor in another part of the city —therefore, *his* car was parked elsewhere and couldn't have been found in the restricted area."

"There you go again—analogies to the rescue when you're in a tight spot!"

"What are the facts? The *gambler* unconsciously wants to *lose*. The success hunter unconsciously wants to *win* and exhausts his psychic masochism in business excitement. They use identical tension in different ways—the gambler unproductively, the businessman productively."

"But——"

"'I'd concocted such a good argument, and now it boomerangs——.' That's what you were going to say, wasn't it?"

The patient was silent for a few moments, then began again, slightly uncertainly: "You can't deny that some businessmen misuse business for gambling purposes."

"True, but they are not the typical successful ones. There is a difference between taking *calculated risks* in business and *gambling* in business. These men you speak of are not businessmen but racketeers disguised as such. Do you claim to be one of them?"

"No, I certainly don't. As a matter of fact"—the patient smiled —"I hate to admit it, but I'm beginning to see what you've been getting at."

The formula: *The gambler unconsciously wants to lose, the success hunter wants unconsciously to win, spending his psychic masochism in business excitement,* defines in general terms the differences between the two.

"For me, gambling is a question posed to Fate: Am I loved?"

"Assuming you were right, why do you challenge Fate time and again?"

"I want to be sure."

Statements of a gambling patient in a winning period

9. GAMBLING: THE TRAGICOMEDY OF IT ALL

The gambler labors under a long series of *quid pro quos*. If these self-deluding fallacies were not associated with real human tragedies, they would be funny. But there is nothing amusing in the contemplation of broken homes, unhappy families, prison terms, or any of the sordid consequences of the gambler's fantasies.

Especially tragic is the fact that the gambler comes more and more to disregard the source of the money he needs for gambling. First he operates with his own money—earnings and savings—and as time goes on, less and less of that money goes to the support of his family and more to gambling. He strains his credit, eventually resorting to the loan shark. Then family funds, business deposits, a client's trust fund are temporarily tapped. The last step in the dreary process is the forging of checks.

The results depend on family indulgence. In the beginning, if it can, the family covers up and pays. But even family allegiance has limits; it must have, in self-defense. Presently the gambler may make the acquaintance of prison routine; if so, he comes out unchanged. Left to his own devices, he simply resumes where he left off: once a gambler, always a gambler. The only possible successful counteraction, psychoanalytic-psychiatric therapy, is at present largely unfamiliar to the public. Recent popularization by national magazines of some of my writings on the psychology of the gambler has started a minimal change, but every new idea has an incubation time of several generations.

Even under the pressure of knowledge that gambling is a neurotic disease, the gambler rarely consults the psychiatrist independently. It is the outraged and desperate family that drags the reluctant addict into the psychiatric consultation room. Here he is at first very penitent and promises co-operation. Those who stick it out have a good prognosis, provided their inner guilt can be mobilized.

Gambling is no respecter of social strata, background, or religion. There is the son of a wealthy businessman, a young man who embezzled money and forged checks many times, each time for a greater amount, while working for different business firms. There is the bartender who lets his family starve while he plays the horses. There is the college professor, not knowing where to turn; so far, his wife and his superiors are ignorant of his debts. There is the lawyer who absconded with his clients' deposits and whose partner is making a last desperate effort to rescue him from gambling. And so on, through a long and tragic procession.

True, dissemination of knowledge concerning gambling as a disease has increased, temporarily, the conflict of some gamblers, so that they may make feeble half attempts to secure help.

I say some, because the majority simply scoff at the idea of psychiatric aid. Those who are sufficiently disturbed to do something about it find a convenient excuse to end by doing nothing. A man telephoned me one day, informed me that he was a gambler from Brooklyn, and requested an answer to his dilemma. This, it developed, consisted of a vicious circle: when in the chips he felt that gambling was a reasonable business; when in a losing period he could not afford costly and protracted psychiatric treatment. Asked for advice, my answer was not too consoling. I told him he would have to break the vicious circle and, when in a winning period, deposit with a reasonable non-gambling friend enough money for treatment, with the proviso that under no condition should the money be returned to him for gambling purposes. The gambler answered indignantly that it couldn't be done and hung up.

A state government executive consulted me in despair. He was at the end of his rope, and had come for consultation because he had heard of my published reports on cured gamblers. He said he had carried around excerpts from one of my published papers for eight months, always postponing calling for an appointment; then he made up his mind that after clearing his desk he would enter treatment with a colleague in his home state, if I would (later) recommend one to him. I never heard from the man again; my first two bills went unpaid and unacknowledged; the third (sent two months after his visit) bore the notation: "Third and last reminder: payment expected within two weeks." This bill was paid and returned with the scribbled remark: "This statement from March 1 arrived; was more revealing than the $ . . . interview." In short, *I* had done *him* an injustice—because he had not paid his bill. By means of this mental sleight of hand the gambler acquired another alibi of injustice. How perfectly the penciled comment mirrored the gambler's typical injustice-collecting by means of self-provoked conflicts!

Big shots and wage earners, people from protected homes sent to exclusive schools, and children left to themselves—all march in the great army of money neurosis, division of gambling. The reason is simple: the baby conflict of undigested megalomania which starts the masochistic ball rolling begins so early in life that later distinctions are still meaningless.

I reproduce parts of a letter written by the scion of a famous family, leaving out all personal or recognizable passages:

Dear Dr. Bergler:

This is a cry for help or advice. This evening, by pure chance, I came across a magazine article on gambling, which repeatedly mentions your name. I read this article just after I had made up my mind "to give up" and to ask the local authorities to prevent me from doing any more harm to myself and all my friends and acquaintances than I have already done in the past months.

The article describes my symptoms so well that I feel there is perhaps some hope of my stopping my mad rush to self-destruction—very much against my own will.

I have in the past year and a half cheated and defrauded my relations, my friends and casual acquaintances of big sums of money, purely to lose it at the various gambling places of Europe. I mean it when I say "to lose it," for I have often won sufficiently large sums to cover my losses at least partially, but I was never satisfied until I lost it all again and went to incredible depths to raise more money to lose it again.

I guess I've always been a gambler, though for years I got over it—at least partially—and now I'm back to it with more determination and more madness than ever before.

For the past few hours, before writing this letter, I have asked myself very seriously whether I'm only writing it in the hope of evading the consequences of my acts. I honestly don't think so. I'm not really afraid of paying for all I have done in my madness. Naturally I keenly feel the disgrace that I've brought upon myself but that too mainly for my children's sake. No, I honestly think I'm really afraid mostly of going on the way I've been going and getting into worse and worse straits and doing greater and greater harm.

I don't know that there is anything you can do from a distance, as it were. I'm not yet ripe for a strait jacket but, if you

ask me, I am ripe to be locked up or put away until I regain my
sanity, if ever.
    I shall do my utmost to keep "it" under control for the next few
months and hope to hear from you in the meantime.

Gambling addiction has other, tangential facets, imbued not
with tragedy but with simple comedy. There is, for example, a
type of gambler who indulges only in harmless gambling; a man
of this type is not a real self-damaging addict but one who can
afford to play for the moderate stakes he chooses and who derives an unconscious pleasure from being upbraided by his partners for silly mistakes in the game. He cashes in on narcissistic
self-humiliation; and although he would deny it, his money losses
—relatively insignificant as they are—contribute mildly to his
harmless masochistic pleasure.

A successful manufacturer in the middle forties came to psychoanalytic treatment by a rather peculiar detour. Wishing to
consult his diagnostician because of varicose veins, he found
that the physician was on vacation and was examined by a substitute, a younger man. The latter asked some questions about
the patient's life. It came out that the patient was completely impotent, and his wife—after fourteen years of marriage—still a
virgin, having married him to support her family and being
frigid and rather puritanical. He, conscious of his impotence, was
in the habit of solving his sexual problem by pressing himself
against young girls in his office, ejaculating without erection.
This idyllic situation was disturbed by the accidental encounter
with the younger physician, who recommended him to me.

The patient proved rather shy and embarrassed; he did not
really want treatment but did not know how to get out of the
quandary he had got into. However, when the question of the
fee came up for discussion, he came quickly to life and energetically (for he felt himself, now, on familiar territory) declared
that it was entirely too much. Obviously he expected me to bargain with him; when he realized that I had no intention of doing
so, he behaved as though my refusal were an immoral action and
complained repeatedly about hard times, high taxes, etc. During

this tirade he kept looking at the analytical couch, avoiding my glance. At last he said in a tone of some disgust: "All right, I'll pay."

I wondered what had caused him to change his mind. Nothing could be elicited from the patient. However, at the beginning of every appointment, as I placed a small paper towel at the head of the couch, he made a curious joke, always with the same laugh: "You have terrible expenses." At first I ignored the joke; then one day I answered: "You're right; every three appointments, from now on, I'm going to put an extra penny on your bill." At last I pressed the point—and discovered that this man, who was totally ignorant concerning psychiatry and had never heard of the institution of the analytic couch, believed the latter to be a part of the medical instrumentarium for curing his potency disturbance. In other words, he assumed that I would provide a prostitute for the purpose of teaching him sex, and that this being so, my fee was not unreasonable after all—since it must cover the cost of this convenience. Disabused of this idea, the patient was very much disappointed and expressed the opinion that there was nothing more to discuss. The situation looked hopeless; the man wanted only to be left alone. He was not interested in changing, nor did he have the slightest understanding of the analytical procedure; every attempt to analyze his conflict produced obvious surprise and revulsion, and it was plain that he kept asking himself "How can I take my leave gracefully?"

Having written him off as unanalyzable, I still thought I would try an experiment. There must be, I told myself, a point at which even this man could be made to become interested in treatment, if one could find it. I started by asking about his hobbies, and learned that he played pinochle. "Are you a good pinochle player?" I inquired. "On the contrary, a very poor one," he replied. "Imagine—here I am a big manufacturer, and I not only make a lot of mistakes at pinochle but I can't even remember the rules." "Do you lose money?" was my next question. "Of course, but that doesn't matter. What gets me is the way my partners kid me about it." "Would you believe in analysis if I could make a good pinochle player out of you?" At this the man became very animated: "Could you really do that? By playing with me?" "No—by analyzing your self-damaging tendencies." Once more he was disappointed. First no prostitute, and now no pinochle. "I hope it is the last disappointment you will experience with me," I said. Having recovered from this second blow, he agreed to treatment on the terms I had outlined. Before very long he became an excellent pinochle player, as evidenced by the fact that his former opponents, recognizing that they had lost a sucker, refused to play with him any longer. Thus having established, in his own words, the superiority and effectiveness of psychiatry, he even consented to treatment for his potency disturbance. . . .

Not every gambler gets off so easily as does this harmless type. In general the gambler's fate is tragic from beginning to end. The basis is always the same: the unconscious wish to lose.[1] Only the rationalizations vary. Gamblers adhere with amazing tenacity to the prevailing fallacy that they can win a fortune. This is the firm belief of every gambler, and if the facts prove exactly the opposite, he decides merely that he is the exception that proves the rule. Discussion on logical grounds gets nowhere with the gambler: a fanatic, defending his masochistic defenses, is immune to common sense. And this fanaticism is unreal whatever the covering cloak.

Doubts of the basic fallacy that it is possible to get rich by gambling are encountered rarely today, even among non-gamblers; they will increase in future with knowledge that gambling is a disease. This, however, will not alter the gamblers; it will simply force them to find new rationalizations. The newest rationalization to come to my ears is that gambling is just a superstitious game of asking Fate whether one is loved. By thus changing a masochistic sickness into a harmless game, the danger is allegedly removed—and, what is more decisive, the old defense perpetuated. What the gambler looks for unconsciously is not love but rejection. His monetary rationalizations are summarized

[1]Gambling is, of course, more complicated clinically than these outlines indicate. For elaboration, see *The Psychology of Gambling*.

in the old story of a man playing a variation of the shell game: in this case his opponent kept his hands behind his back, holding in one of them a silver dollar. In order to win, the man had to guess which hand held the dollar; if he guessed wrong, he lost. An onlooker, seeing that the opponent was cheating by manipulating the coin from hand to hand after the guess had been made, started to warn the victim. The latter indignantly interrupted him: "Do you think I'm blind? *I* know he's cheating, and I'm not going to play with him, but first I have to win back my money." This is a perfect picture of the typical gambler.

The connection between gambling and investing money on Wall Street by innocent suckers was illustrated by an incident which occurred a few years ago when a certain Wall Street employee was called up for jury duty in a gambling case, and finding it inconvenient to serve, tried to get out of it with the excuse: "I'm in the gambling business myself." This indiscrete statement cost him his job, though he was later rehired. Fred Schwed based his delightful Wall Street satire, *Where Are the Customers' Yachts?* on the joke about the newcomer to New York who, after having been taken on a tour of Wall Street and shown the bankers' and brokers' yachts lying in the East River, innocently asked: "And where are the customers' yachts?" Mr. Schwed distinguished between investment and speculation as follows: speculation tries to make a great deal of money out of a small amount of money; investment tries to prevent a great deal of money from becoming a small amount of money.

Well, "the time of wonderful nonsense," as a journalist once called the roaring twenties, is far from past—the tendency of the sucker to part with his money is always with us. According to Benjamin Stolberg, his prototype is "the man who goes into Wall Street on a shoestring and loses his shoes when he tries to save the string."

PART FOUR: GOLDDIGGER AND PLAYBOY, INC.

It is difficult enough to acquire fame. It is impossible to change its nature once you've acquired it. No, you can never ruin an architect by proving that he's a bad architect. But you can ruin him because he's an atheist, or because somebody sued him, or because he slept with some woman, or because he pulls wings off bottleflies. You'll say it doesn't make sense? Of course it doesn't. That's why it works. Reason can be fought with reason. How are you going to fight the unreasonable? The trouble with you, my dear, and with most people, is that you don't have sufficient respect for the sense- less. The senseless is the major factor in our lives.[1] *You have no chance if it is your enemy. But if you can make it become your ally—ah, my dear!* . . .*

Toohey in The Fountainhead, by AYN RAND

10. AN EMOTIONAL CRIPPLE SELLS HIS LOOKS

The golddigger's position on the marriage market corresponds exactly to that of the streetwalker on the prostitution market; each sells her body and charm in a cold-blooded business deal. Each must use conscious hypocrisy in order to disguise her aims—the prostitute less, the golddigger more. Both are on the market of feelings for cash.

Nobody likes to be cheated on the market of feelings. Men are frightened of golddiggers, women of playboys. Everyone sees the golddigger and the

[1]Words set in roman indicate author's emphasis.

playboy purely and simply as cold-blooded crooks, actuated by a single-minded evil determination to catch, hook, and drain the victim. They are conceded no other feelings. When one comes to examine it, the naïve single-mindedness with which such people are attributed is, of course, absurd. Even a crook—in fact, especially a crook—has an unconscious psychology of his own. The question is, what made him (or her) a crook? In view of the universal fear of the ominous firm of Golddigger & Playboy, Incorporated, a psychiatric examination is justified in a study of money neurosis.

In a long series of cases I have observed that the *conscious* aim of both—to be supported, if possible on a grand scale—is counteracted by *unconscious* forces, resulting in a severe emotional conflict. Many of these neurotics—and both the male and the female of the species are invariably severely neurotic—were capable of achieving their conscious aim temporarily, only to find themselves depressed, dissatisfied, bored, or, even worse from their point of view, drawn into escapades endangering their newly achieved status of respectability. Others labored under a more grotesque conflict: despite their determination to hook a victim for purposes of exploitation, they attached themselves to the wrong people and found themselves cheated out of their conscious aim.

A good-looking woman in her early twenties consulted me because of a problem which she phrased by asking: "Please tell me frankly whether or not you consider me crazy."

"What makes you suspect that you may be psychotic?"

"Everyone tells me it's crazy to have two apartments when I'm not able to afford it. You see, I'm divorced; my husband left me the apartment in the Bronx, and it's a nice place—but men don't respect a girl unless she has a smart address."

"What kind of men?"

"Men of means. I can't respect a man without money."

"I see. And what about your second apartment?"

"Well, I've discovered over and over that men don't respect you unless you live in a high-class neighborhood, so I rented a room from a family on Park Avenue. Very nice people—I'm considered a sort of distant relative."

"Did having two addresses improve your social status?"

"Oh, I don't admit to the apartment in the Bronx. Yes, it increased the respect of the set of people I try to mingle with. The trouble is, I spend my entire income—I'm a fairly well-paid minor executive—on these damned apartments and can't afford the slightest luxury."

"Why did you divorce your husband?"

"I couldn't respect him any more."

"Did he lose his money?"

"He never made money. You see, I had an unhappy home life. Father and mother were very simple people without any ambition. I fought with father for years, trying to convince him that he must refurnish the living room, because otherwise I couldn't entertain girl friends and young men who might be prospective husbands. After eight years I finally won that battle. Eventually I married an immature boy from a comparatively wealthy family. I knew how weak he was but I believed I could manage him. We set him up in business. Well, he was a complete flop—he overspent, he had no ambition. I lost respect for him and got a divorce."

"Were you ever in love with him?"

"I couldn't love a man I didn't respect. Anyhow I guess I married him mainly because I was unhappy at home."

"What did you get out of this marriage?"

"I have a nice apartment, if that's what you mean."

"I meant, what did you get out of it emotionally?"

"Nothing. I couldn't respect my husband—and that was that."

"And now you are determined to marry a wealthy man?"

"A man whom I can respect."

"I see."

"Do you think I'm crazy?"

"No. In pursuit of your debatable aim of marrying for money, you simply made, with your two apartments, a concession to the foolishness and snobbishness of these men whom you call 'prospective husbands.'"

"I'm glad to hear that. Then you consider me completely normal?"

"Not at all. I consider you a neurotic who is obviously incapable of loving anyone."

"Do you mean you think I should marry for love and not for money?"

"That alternative doesn't exist for you. You are incapable of love."

"What do you want me to do—live on a pauper's income all my life?"

"I have just answered your question. *Within the framework of your neurosis,* you have made some kind of adjustment—provided you achieve your aim."

"What do you mean?"

"Well, you were not too successful in your first choice of a husband. What guarantee have you that you won't repeat the mistake?"

"Then you suspect that I'm a flop even there?"

"It seems to me that your conscious aim of golddigging is counteracted by a self-damaging, though *unconscious,* tendency."

"I want to remain poor? Never!"

"How do you explain the fact that you picked a man whom you could neither manage nor respect?"

The young lady began to cry, and admitted that she had consulted me because the same thought had occurred to her while she was reading my book, *Divorce Won't Help.* She suspected that she *would* repeat the mistake of her first marriage.

"How can I protect myself?" she asked.

"Against what?"

"Against marrying the wrong man."

"You'll have to clarify your aim. Do you want to become a better golddigger or an emotionally stable, normal person?"

"I resent that word golddigger."

"What would you suggest as a synonym?"

"I told you, I can't respect a man without ambition."

"Whom are you kidding?"

"O.K., O.K. What shall I do? Would you suggest treatment?"

"Psychoanalysis cannot make you a better golddigger."

"What *can* it do for me?"

"Under favorable circumstances, treatment could restore your ability to feel and think like a human being. At the moment you are only a calculating machine."

"And one with a flaw——"

"One with a flaw, as your marriage proved."

"Have you ever encountered a case like mine?"

"You are very far from being an exception. The golddiggers I see are for the most part women who have achieved their conscious aim of mink coat-and-penthouse luxury. After a time they find themselves bored, dissatisfied and depressed. They start dangerous escapades, get frightened and want treatment."

"But there *are* women who want to use analysis for becoming better golddiggers?"

"Of course. They're playing with fire—when their money neurosis is removed, there is danger that they will reject their previous aim."

"Does that always happen?"

"Not at all. Some leave analysis after the attachment to the lover evaporates. Some interrupt treatment at that point with the abstruse statement that they can't afford normalcy now that it has endangered their marriage of convenience."

"I wish I were that far along!"

"Obviously your self-damaging tendencies are stronger than those of the ladies I described."

"What will happen to me?"

"I suspect that, with your cynicism, you will remarry for money —and with the second husband's money enter analysis in order to prevent a third fiasco."

"A pleasant prospect!"

"Well, what do you suggest?"

"I'll rent my apartment and go into analysis now."

"To become a better golddigger or a better wife and happier person?"

"I want to be happy."

"Neurosis and conscious happiness don't mix."

"I found that out the hard way."

The playboy is the golddigger's male counterpart. He, too, believes that the world owes him a luxurious living, which it is his right to receive, not as a result of work but as payment for his sex appeal. A man of this type consulted me because of depression and drinking too much. He had tried repeatedly to stop drinking, without success. It developed that he considered his slight alcoholic addiction a threat to his commercialized marriage plans. However, he did not admit to the real reason at first but only said he couldn't afford the reputation of a drinker.

He was twenty-seven years old and twice divorced, but did not consider his two marital fiascos unusual. In fact, he had not consulted me with any thought of clearing up the marital difficulties but simply to be cured of his alcoholism.

"What is your profession?" I asked him.

"I've worked in different fields," he answered evasively.

"For instance?"

"Well, first I went to college. After college, I looked around ——"

"Looking for what?"

"For a position. I became engaged to a girl whose father owned a big iron manufacturing outfit, and after we were married I finally went to work in her father's office."

"What does the word 'finally' allude to?"

"The girl had an independent income from her grandmother's estate. I figured that there was no need for me to work. We traveled and had a good time for a while, but then, under her father's influence, she began insisting that I go to work. I wasn't too happy over the prospect—who cares about iron anyway?—but I finally gave in. Unfortunately, our drinking interfered with my work. How can anybody work with a hang-over?"

"What did your first wife want from you? Did she want you to be a drinking companion or a hard worker?"

"That's just it—you get the point. I told her, either you let me work, in which case you dispense with a companion in your luxury life, or you let me get out of that stupid office so we can have a good time."

"Did she understand what you meant?"

"Well, you know how these wealthy girls are. She upbraided me and accused me of being a playboy and a parasite. She was a parasite herself, but when I pointed that out, she said: 'Nobody expects a wealthy girl to work—with a man it's different.' Did you ever hear such nonsense?"

"And the end?"

"That *was* the end. She divorced me after I failed to show up at that stupid office for a few days. These bitches are just unreasonable. She was the one who'd promoted the spree we went on—then she called me a playboy and left. I think her old fool of a father gave her the idea. She got rid of me just to cover up her own drinking."

"What happened sexually in the marriage?"

"She was a cold fish—though she accused *me* of coldness. She began an affair with another man and later married him. To my satisfaction, that marriage went on the rocks too."

"And you?"

"I was left out in the cold. After some time I got hooked up with another girl in her set. But it was the same old story—this time the family owned a big shipyard. I had to learn something new, and I'll admit I wasn't too good at it. The girl didn't drink so much, but she was insanely jealous."

"Did you give her cause for jealousy?"

"Well, I'm not claiming I married her for love. But she just believed she owned me. She began to be really violent and eventually went to Reno. I wouldn't repeat the things she called me. All I can say is, when you marry a wealthy girl you marry nothing but stinginess and complaints."

"Why *did* you marry for money?"

"I didn't, exactly. I just never had too much confidence in my ability to work hard. I like a good time, and imagined that these wealthy women would be glad to get a good-looking husband. But what did I get out of the deal? Nothing but the reputation of a playboy. Those two bitches made an alcoholic out of me—I had to drink to forget the troubles they caused me."

"And now?"

"Well, I managed to save a little money——"

"How?"

"I got wise to my second wife's tricks early in the game, and I had an idea that the trip to Reno was coming eventually. So I managed to save some of *her* money—you know, little gifts and so on."

"I see."

"Nothing spectacular, you understand. She was furious when she found out—she threatened me with the law, and I countered by threatening her with a scandal she couldn't afford."

"All in all, not too successful a business venture."

"Reasonably successful—taking the hard times into account."

"And now?"

"Now I'm through with that crowd of wealthy parasites. All they want is a good time, but if a fellow gives it to them they get full of moral indignation and call him a playboy. And if he doesn't, they call him a washout. It's a hard world."

"Have you ever considered the possibility of supporting yourself?"

"What are my chances? A fifty-dollar-a-week job? I haven't got a good head for business. Can I help it?"

"Is your prospective *third* wife already in the picture?"

"No, I'm wise to the whole gang now and I want to enjoy my freedom as long as I can—meaning as long as my money holds out."

"Why do you want to get rid of your drinking habit?"

"Well, you figure that one out for me."

"I have figured it out. It's a prerequisite for the next marriage deal."

"You can only sell what you have, you know. In my case that happens to be looks and personality."

"No illusions about yourself?"

"Not any more. A few years ago I had some, but those nice consoling thoughts evaporated."

"And what remained?"

"A correct evaluation of my chances. You can call it cynicism or cold-blooded calculation if you want to—I'm immune to that kind of criticism. The point is to get the best out of a poor deal."

"Has it occurred to you that you are emotionally sick? That your attitude bars you from all the feelings that give color to life?"

"Don't give me that stuff. I don't believe in any romantic nonsense about love."

"Apparently it hasn't dawned on you that an analysis of your overdrinking must, out of inner necessity, include an analysis of your whole personality. And that changing the latter may endanger your ideas of marriage and sex as a business proposition involving buying-and-selling commodities."

"Look, Doc, let's face facts. I don't need any face-lifting or morale-building job. I want you to remove my drinking compulsion, that's all. Everything else will take care of itself—and believe me, there's nothing a good-sized bank account can't cure."

"You said a little while ago that you're immune to criticism, meaning reproach. You will find out that you are very sensitive to inner reproaches: your drinking and depression are intimately connected with that."

"You don't say."

"And you'll discover that your cynicism is no less explainable psychologically than your emotional dearth."

"Just do your job and we'll get along fine."

"I'm telling you just for the record. I'll remind you, one day, of my warning."

"Don't worry, I'll give it to you in writing that you 'warned' me."

These two sick people had several clues in common. Both the golddigger and the playboy were firmly convinced of their right to be supported, giving in exchange their sex appeal. They did not feel that they robbed others; on the contrary, they became indignant on finding that their marriage partners were unwilling simply to hand over the bank roll.

The cynical approach was predominant, more openly in the man than in the girl, who still operated on the basis of being unable to respect a man without money. When cornered she made no attempt to deny her golddigging, though she went through the motions of being offended. Both found work, in the usual meaning of the word, distasteful, and felt no obligation to work to support themselves. Neither considered the marital sale, so to speak, of their sex organs to be prostitution. Remnants of conscious scruples were disclaimed because of the fantasy that they did the partner a favor.

Both were exclusively concerned with improving their parasitic tendencies, partly rationalized by the wish to move in "higher social circles." Normal feelings were rejected as silly and romantic. Both were at bottom neurotically depressed people, though they denied it. The most amazing fact about them was, of course, the complete conviction of being justified in their behavior, coupled with an "iron will" to achieve the position of being supported without work.

Adherents of the belief that money is everything will be surprised to learn that cleverness in the realm of feelings does not pay off. The question of whether to marry for love or money does not arise in the case of golddiggers and playboys, simply because they are incapable of normal feelings of love. What appears to be a consciously arrived-at decision is but a secondary attempt to capitalize on a neurotic defect.

They are thus cheated cheaters. No injustice is done them, but no one wastes pity on them either: all the pity and compassion goes to the innocent victim. However, the victim is less innocent than appearances indicate. He is not caught because of the cleverness of the cheater but because inner neurotic tendencies make him the prey of a neurotic allure.

Romantic love is for fools.

Motto of the golddigger and the playboy

11. EMOTIONAL COLDNESS ON THE MARKET OF FEELINGS

The most conspicuous characteristic of golddiggers and playboys is their emotional coldness. For them, feelings are something to be faked. They go through the act of sexual intercourse in a purely mechanical way. Both seem incapable of any real or decent emotions. The only time they show real emotion is when they are airing their grievances, complaining of how unjustly they are treated by others. These grievances, like those of all golddiggers and playboys, may be summed up in the phrase: "I don't get enough."

A surrealist artist allowed his wife to support him for years. Although her income was turned over to him promptly every month, he continually complained of her stinginess. Finally she divorced him. Infuriated, he nevertheless wasted no time in marrying another woman, also a provider but on a reduced scale. Later he tried persistently to start an affair with his first wife—with a view to obtaining double support, as his money demands proved. The ex-wife being unreceptive, he began, completely oblivious of his own neurotic behavior, to accuse her friends of cruelty, blaming them for her financial inaccessibility.

The appetite for getting appears to be insatiable in golddiggers and playboys. The first and rather obvious conclusion to be drawn is that they are parasites: they want to be fed, and well fed. Their social, sartorial, jewel-devouring appetites seem at first glance to be overdimensional. If the problem were really so simple, the solution would be equally simple—to give them what they want. But this experiment has been performed—involuntarily—innumerable times by their victims, and invariably they remained dissatisfied.

A golddigger married a wealthy manufacturer, from whom she soon began to extract promises of jewelry, furs, trips, etc., before and during intercourse. The passive husband acceded to these demands, but began to grow angry when she continued to reproach him for his stinginess. He thought he saw a resemblance between his wife's behavior and that of a prostitute; and to test the suspicion, he started to have an affair with a semi-prostitute—ostensibly to observe her technique of money demands. At first the girl, perhaps sensing that she could get more from him if she let him take the initiative, made no such demands, but eventually, growing impatient, she showed her true colors. His dossier completed, the manufacturer demanded a divorce from his wife. She agreed to give it to him—for a fabulous sum; and threatened, if the money were not forthcoming, to make public the facts of his (nonexistent) potency disturbance and his quite real income tax secrets. In the end he bought her off, thoroughly disgusted with women. It did not occur to him that he had *chosen* this type of

woman for the purpose of satisfying his real unconscious wish—
to be kicked around.

A naïve onlooker could conclude that the golddigger and the
playboy are obsessed by a getting-wish which merely increases
with every fulfillment.

The question also arises: what causes the parasitic tendency to
be put into operation? Why does one adult individual want to
give and another to get? The first opening in the parasite's unconscious armor is his constant dissatisfaction. Give him as much
as you can and he will still feel unjustly treated.

A writer, supported for years by his wealthy wife, lived with
her in a constant state of feud. She irritated him to the point of
exasperation by her spending sprees. Though he told himself she
was free to do as she liked with her own money, her spending
made him furious. He could not complain of the standard of living
she offered him; his social and material needs were well taken
care of. He admitted that his feeling of being cheated out of
money was irrational. This, however, did not prevent him from
cherishing the grudge against his wife. By way of retaliation for
the irritation she caused him, he visited prostitutes, paid them
with his wife's money, got drunk with them, and gave them sex,
which he refused to his wife.

The parasite is a psychic masochist. He does not want to get
—that is only his conscious aim. Unconsciously he wants to be
refused. The adult who constantly expresses a strong wish for
social and financial "security" should be satisfied when he has
achieved these aims. If instead he is still dissatisfied, the expressed wish is but a camouflage for something deeper and repressed. This is the situation with the golddigger and playboy.
If they don't get, they feel unjustly treated. If they do get, they
again feel unjustly treated—because they didn't get enough.

One might ask why, if these neurotics really want to be refused,
they don't achieve their curious aim in a simple way. This is a
sensible question, but unfortunately common sense is not the
currency of the unconscious personality. The latter works on the
principle of *wishes, guilt, defenses. Repressed wishes are coun-*

*teracted by inner guilt: the result is that an inner defense
mechanism, an alibi, must be built up.*

Apply this rule to golddiggers and playboys, and you arrive at
the paradoxical formula: *what these neurotics unconsciously want
is refusal. Unconscious guilt pertaining to that strange self-damaging aim forces them secondarily to furnish an unconscious alibi.
That alibi is insatiable greed, secondarily permeating consciousness.*

The behavior of all three of the people described in this chapter is, from a realistic viewpoint, completely irrational. The
writer was aware of this himself, though his theoretical knowledge did not prevent his being, unconsciously, an injustice-collector, nor did it stop him from revenging himself on his wife by
paying prostitutes with her money. The artist might have considered that his wife could give him no more than the trust fund
provided, and that in handing over the monthly checks she was
doing her utmost, but this thought did not, of course, enter his
mind. His conscious theory was that you have to keep these
women in submission. He satisfied the masochistic unconscious
wishes of his wife but ended by making his demands unen-
durable even to her, as her final slave rebellion proved. It was
impossible for him to comprehend the shift from him to another
deposition of self-torture, and he blamed her acquaintances for
the divorce. The wife of the manufacturer might more sensibly
have chosen a more propitious time for making her demands and
thus avoided implanting in her husband's mind the comparison
with a paid prostitute, but obviously her behavior was not dictated by common sense.

All three people were insatiable, dissatisfied, demanding, reproachful. All golddiggers, they were at the same time their own
—maritally speaking—grave diggers.

Golddiggers of both sexes are psychic masochists with an added
peculiarity: the defensive layer of coldness is reinforced. Since
we do not possess an apparatus for measuring unconscious tendencies quantitatively, we must base our conclusions on the thickness of the unconsciously produced defense in relation to the
thickness of warded-off tendencies. Judging from the emotional

coldness (which represents the defense), the masochistic layer must be massive.

The emotional coldness and frigidity serves another purpose as well; it denies the existence of feelings in the first place. The inner defense runs something like this: "How could I ever have been masochistically attached if I cannot feel at all?" With this trick is fashioned another facet of the alibi before the inner conscience.

One might also suspect that this coldness expresses a reversal of the childhood situation. At that point the individual felt coldly rejected by his upbringers. Later in life, he (or she) reverses the roles and treats his victim coldly. The suspicion is justified; it pertains, however, only to superficial defensive layers.

There exists further incontestable clinical proof of the psychic-masochistic substructure of golddiggers and playboys. This can be seen in their choice of lovers—without exception mean, cruel, brutal persons. The woman who, in her marriage of gilded convenience, is no more than a calculating machine inevitably is drawn to the uncouth and brutal lover and to the humiliating situation. Then, typically, she gets into difficulties that endanger her financial and social "security." The same holds true for the playboy. Without feeling and a cheat in marriage, he becomes an easy prey to the shrewish and calculating girl friend. Here again the roles are reversed.

One of the shrewdest golddiggers I analyzed was a beautiful young woman of French extraction married to an overaged millionaire. She consulted me because, as she expressed it, she was slipping. With complete cynicism she related that she had married for money and social position, disclosing without any inhibition the game she played of making the old fool jealous and then, with skillful timing, reassuring him. She invented adventures in order to frighten him, denying their reality as soon as she had succeeded in working him into a state near a heart attack. Personally she did not believe that pleasure in sex was possible for women. Bored to death with her life as an elderly millionaire's wife, she had started an affair with her husband's young secretary, a good-looking nobody. It then developed that the nobody was leading a double life: submissive at his job, he was a primitive person, priding himself as a seducer of women. The patient found herself insanely jealous of his many affairs and went through veritable hell, aware even as she suffered of a wave of surprise at her own ability to have such feelings. Heretofore she had considered herself to be *above* feeling, and, as she was frank to admit, had thought that money was everything. "And here," she exclaimed indignantly, "I find that money *isn't!*"

Amusingly enough, it was the lover whom she wanted to send into treatment "to make him acceptable to me." I ironically reminded her of her shattered motto: "Money is all." I pointed out that she obviously harbored a great deal of self-torturing material and suggested that she would do well to get rid of it. She entered treatment and quickly came to understand her masochistic difficulties; she even confessed that the lover had started to extort money from her, a circumstance all the more infuriating because it virtually amounted to supporting the other women. Still, she was helpless against the young man for some time. Later, under pressure of analysis and partly as a result of the patient's half shifting of her masochistic attitude, the affair was dissolved. She then declared herself cured, whereas I was convinced that she had simply given up an untenable position to shift her pleasure-displeasure pattern to some other point. At first, something strange happened: she became uninterested in *all* men, concentrating her interest on sculpture. She had some small talent in that direction, but her artistic products were ghosted by experts. Since she was wealthy, it was no problem to arrange for an exhibition of her works; she, however, wanted real recognition, and to that end attached herself to a famous art critic, who teased her without mercy. He continually promised connections, but never kept his promises, which infuriated her. As she always called me up when in trouble—each time asking for *one* appointment—I was able to observe her during the course of these pitched battles. After a few cynical revulsions she became pitifully discouraged—"I'm a sexual washout, so why not take advantage of being a woman?" —and began a series of directed affairs, as she called them; directed, that is, toward recognition via bed. Masochistically she

perpetually chose the wrong protectors, eating her heart out because of encountering so much ingratitude.

This woman, who had handled her husband with artistry, was
helpless when confronted with a brutal teaser or a brutal situation. It took her a still longer time to see through, and half change,
her masochistic antics. She refused to finish her treatment—
postponing it until some time *after* her husband's death.

One question has been left unanswered: the specificity of financial sponging. There are many ways of elaborating on a masochistic conflict; why does the golddigger choose—in addition to
the *two-steps* technique of cruelty and coldness toward the mate
plus submission to a cruel and cold lover—also a second elaboration, the financial exploitation of the mate?

With monotonous regularity, in dozens of analyses of golddiggers and playboys, I have found this infantile elaboration: the
child felt, whether justifiable or not, unjustly treated (exaggerated demands in a normal household have the same results as
genuine denial of affection to the child, for neurosis is an elaboration of infantile fantasy, not a copy of reality) and became
stabilized on the masochistic level. The same child who accused
his mother, inwardly, of coldness nevertheless witnessed excited
quarrels connected with money. The inner conclusion drawn by
the child was that his mother (father) had feelings—but only
about money. Thus money became a weapon in the battle of feelings, and led, in later life, to the formula: "I shall take away what
you love most: money."

In seasons of pestilence, some of us will have a secret attraction to the disease—a terrible passing inclination to die of it. And all of us have like wonders hidden in our breasts, only needing circumstances to evoke them.

DICKENS, *A Tale of Two Cities*

12. MOTH AND FLAME

To attempt to sell in the stock market or commodity exchanges something one didn't possess or was incapable of delivering on order on a specific date would get one into a good deal of trouble. But on the emotional market lack of feelings is a commodity highly valued: the golddigger of either sex officially sells faked feelings; in *inner reality* his or her coldness is precisely the lure that attracts a certain neurotic type of victim as magically as a burning light attracts moths.

Who are these victims? The male victim of the

golddigger is, without exception, a psychic masochist who unconsciously feeds, in this way, his appetite for injustice-collecting.
Consciously, of course, he wants all the good things love can offer:
real warmth, real mutual interest, real companionship. Unconsciously he wants just the opposite—and how bitterly he complains, afterward, when his wife turns out to be a cold and calculating golddigger! Monotonously one asks the salient question:
"Why didn't your instinct forewarn you?" and gets the invariable
excited answer: "I just didn't know. How could I?" It is useless
to remind him that the normal person knows intuitively.

The playboy's victim is a female counterpart of this individual—
a psychic masochist who, like him, wishes only a provider of injustices to satisfy her craving for injustice-collecting. Hence the
commiseration bestowed on the victims of golddiggers and playboys is superfluous. Both have got what they wanted, unconsciously. True, objectively it appears that they are involved in
tragedy—as they are, if their situation is measured by the yardstick of conscious pursuit of happiness. But the brand of happiness preferred by these neurotics is not visible on the surface.
Nothing happens by *chance* in the emotional life—*there are no
innocent victims of wrecked marriages.*

Here are a few examples of this type of neurotic:

A big businessman in the early forties consulted me, as he put
it, in desperation. "You see in me a complete failure," he began.
"True, if you were to ask my bank, look at my income tax return
or consult Dun & Bradstreet, you'd get a different picture, but
what good does my financial success do? I'm the victim of a
calculating shrew who's tormented me for years. And the worst
of it is, I'm desperately in love with her and utterly incapable of
getting rid of her."

"More details, please."

"Well, what it boils down to is that I'm married to a woman
with no more feelings than a marble statue. But you wanted details . . . I'm a self-made man. My background was poor—simple
people who worked hard to make the barest living. Father and
mother ran a small store, and the children had to help. I'm the
oldest of four boys. I remember crying bitterly because I was

neglected and life seemed such a burden. Mother never had time for me—or for herself, for that matter. It took me a long time to understand what a poor slave she really was; as a child I took her preoccupation with work for malicious indifference to me. I felt completely alone. Father was a worrier and never really cared for us children. I ran away from home at fourteen.

"I worked as a messenger boy, dishwasher and so on—the usual 'rags to riches' story, getting a little better job each time until finally, in my middle twenties, I started to make good. I was thrifty, never spent a nickel on luxury—my puritanical ancestors seemed to hold council every time I was tempted to spend a little money, and their advice was always the same: don't splurge, don't debauch. I don't know why they didn't say: don't live— maybe because *living* meant working fourteen hours a day."

"And your emotional needs?"

"Never made themselves felt. Work and dreaming up the ideal wife of the future were enough for me. Would you believe that at the age of twenty-nine I was still a virgin? Once, after a stag party, I went out with one of the girls, but I was so revolted I nearly vomited. I decided then that to satisfy the puritan in me I would have to marry before I could have a sex life—otherwise my guilty conscience would make me miserable. Of course, I had it all figured out in my fantasy: my wife must be kind, loving, understanding, and full of admiration for me."

"Did you find your dream girl?"

"I found a *caricature* of the dream girl—though I mistook the imitation for pure gold. She played her part admirably. I met her at a party and she captivated me at once by letting me spend half an hour explaining some successful business venture. I was rather shy with women, and she undoubtedly sensed that the only way to get on firm ground was to let me talk about my business, so she skillfully brought the conversation around to it. You understand, I only realized that much later—at the time I believed I had made a real hit. I didn't realize then either that it was her casual way of talking about sex that gave me the feeling of dealing with a woman of the world. She said something about a disappointing experience with a brutal man—which immediately made me want to protect her. I've got to give her credit: she sized me up correctly and capitalized on my shyness, letting me believe I was *the* real man. Even though I'm the victim of her calculating coldness, I've never stopped admiring her for her shrewdness. She did a fine psychological confidence job."

"So you felt, when you first became acquainted with your wife, that you had met your dream girl?"

"An improved edition, if that were possible. She was divorced, and lived in a good hotel, allegedly on some small allowance. Later the truth came out: she was practically an adventuress, and—until I stepped into the picture—at the end of her rope. Of course, as I told you, all this was unknown to me before my precipitate marriage."

"Were there any warning signs?"

"Sure, but I didn't pay any attention to them. I was madly in love—I married her a few weeks after meeting her. And my marriage has been hell—emotional hell. Right from the beginning my wife was cold and indifferent. Why she acted that way, without even a pretense of feeling, I never quite understood. It was as if she were just out to humiliate me, deliberately; in bed, at meals, even in company. For instance, if we were with a group of people and the conversation turned to some actor's sex appeal and my wife said, apparently without any connection but very pointedly that *I* was good at making money—well, the implication there is pretty obvious."

"Did your wife have any reason for disparaging your sex ability?"

"Yes and no. I needed her help—which she gave condescendingly, sometimes with disdain. She was cold; when I wanted her, I had to beg on my knees, literally and figuratively. There was one specific situation, though, in which I acted—well, paradoxically. It's so shameful and humiliating——"

"It will do you good to unburden yourself. I suspect that you've never confessed to anyone what a mess you got into maritally."

"That's true."

"There is no shame involved—just neurotic illness—in your strange tolerance of what usually is not tolerated."

"Thanks. Maybe you're right, and not just trying to console me. In any case, things went so far that I even tolerated her affairs with other men—and what men! Would you believe it, that cold, calculating woman was an absolute sucker for men who were even colder and more calculating than she was—impossible people, half gigolo, half parasite. She even supported them, gave them money—my money."

"How did you find out?"

"I got anonymous letters and engaged a detective. When I confronted her with the evidence, my charming wife claimed that my wishy-washy attitude in sex made it imperative for her to have affairs. 'Imperative' was actually the word she used. Well, that was hitting below the belt directly at the weakest point, and she scored 100 per cent. All my raving and threatening was met with a cool: 'What did you expect?' "

"When was that?"

"Two years after my marriage. Seven years ago, to be exact."

"And for seven years you have tolerated, condoned, paid for your wife's lovers?"

At this the patient began to shed tears of self-pity, and then went on to complete the picture of complete self-humiliation by admitting that his wife's unfaithfulness had served, for some reason, to increase his sexual attachment to her. "I know it's crazy, but it happened. And that's not all. Her main lover was married to a wealthy woman from the Social Register; he was a gambler who needed more money than his wife gave him—or than he could extract. So he obtained a second provider—myself, through the medium of my wife. After the blowup, I asked her to stop seeing that particular man. She promised—without, of course, ever keeping the promise—to stop her affair with him, but insisted that we continue our friendship with him and his wife. You see, she was a snob, and the man's wife had excellent social connections. Well, the result was that I was forced to endure the man's company two or three evenings every week."

"What was your wife's argument for that peculiar arrangement?"

"She claimed that her boy friend's wife was ignorant of what had been going on and would become suspicious if we stopped seeing them. I really believe she just wanted to torture me—though it was true that she didn't want to lose the friendship of the man's socially prominent wife."

"Were you neighbors? If so, why didn't you move somewhere else? New York is a big city."

"We live in Westchester, and yes, we're neighbors. Of course I wanted to sell the estate, but my wife objected."

"Then this thing is still going on?"

"Yes."

"What kind of personality has your wife's lover?"

"He's a brutal, parasitic guy who cares for nothing but gambling. His brutality is responsible for his hold on my wife: he treats her like dirt—and from him, she takes it. That's the thing that burns me up. *She* treats *me* like dirt, and is treated the same way herself by another man!"

"I presume that you have tried, unsuccessfully, to imitate his behavior?"

"How did you know? Yes, I tried—and she laughed in my face."

"Do you understand that your being mistreated is not just by chance?"

"I guess so. I feel sick and humiliated. The bottom fell out of my world when I finally realized what a mess I must be, to go on taking punishment like that for so long. It *can't* go on any longer. I want treatment, if you think I have a chance."

The story of the male victim's female counterpart involves a distinguished-looking woman in the early thirties, of well-bred and cultured background.

"I am really horrified at the miserable conflict I have to tell you about," she began. "Moreover, I'm ashamed—and not out of prudishness. I made a terrible fool of myself, and now I can't get out of the net that was thrown over me."

"Would you care to be more specific?"

"Yes—I'll have to be. Three years ago I married my second husband—my first marriage had ended in a divorce court in Florida. My second husband impressed me as charming, witty, and slightly adventurous. I loved that quality in him, which is natural, considering my conservative upbringing. He seemed to know all about everything, he had a worldly, attractively ironic outlook on life, and he was a good sport. Looking back, I'd say I looked up to him as a schoolgirl might look up to a movie star."

"You had gone through a first marriage and yet were still so naïve?"

"My first marriage was a terrible mistake. It lasted only a few months. The man I married turned out to be an impostor who got into some sort of trouble and one day disappeared, absconding with a great amount of money from my estate. He never showed up again—and I simply didn't care."

"Really?"

"Well, after some time anyway. My family consoled me by saying that anyone can make a mistake."

"Was your impostor-like first husband also charming and confidence-inspiring?"

The lady said in surprise: "Why, yes, how did you know?"

"Impostors of that type generally are—it's a part of their stock in trade."

"I met him in Mexico, and my family was as much taken in as I was. Well, after the divorce I made up my mind to be more careful next time. Obviously these crooks prey on rich girls, so I knew I must watch out."

"Did you watch out?"

"I did. I even rather overdid it, suspecting *all* men of evil designs. But that wore off after a while and I tried to strike a happy medium by carefully distinguishing between true and false."

"This happy medium failed you in choosing your second husband?"

"That's the real tragedy! It's all right for a young girl to make a silly mistake, but for a mature woman to *repeat* the mistake in spite of experience——"

The lady's brave objectivity was all on the surface; she cried bitterly and hopelessly, and it was not the crying of one who had been hurt but that of an irreparably damaged human being.

"I found a letter written by my second husband's—well, do you call it girl friend or sweetheart? The letter was written in filthy language, quoting my husband's own disgusting expressions. I don't mean sexy but really filthy. I was referred to several times in such phrases as 'rich cow.' It was obvious that the pair had teamed up long ago and that I was just an object of exploitation. Words cannot describe what I felt; words are a poor medium for expressing feelings. What it came down to was that I was supporting my husband's real love—if you can use the word 'love' about a relationship in which the woman holds a whip and the man takes whipping gladly."

"When and how did you come into possession of the incriminating letter?"

"I found it in a suit pocket when I was giving some clothes to the cleaner. Why he left it there is beyond me—perhaps he didn't really care what I felt."

"Why do you avoid mentioning the time of your discovery?"

"Because all my humiliation and degradation hang on the time element. I found the letter two years ago—and I am still married to my husband."

"Did you confront him with what you had discovered?"

"Yes—he slapped me and called me a dirty spy! I told him he was a parasite, that his real-estate business was just front, that he lived on me and supported his girl at my expense. I *told* him—— But I'm still his wife, two years later. I took all that, and more. I cannot leave him even though I know that to him I am just a 'wealthy cow' tolerated simply because I provide him with everything."

"What, in your opinion, is his hold on you?"

"It's a sort of magnetism. I'm just incapable of breaking away. I've decided to finish it all—well, hundreds of times. But I don't. Often he's told me, cynically, that some men need two women; I know that's all lies and exploitation, but I'm helpless as a rabbit hypnotized by a snake."

Contradictions are mainly missing links in our slightly irrational thinking. Contradictions denote our inability to conceive the coexistence of variegated inner defenses, kaleidoscopically arranged. Of course, it is easier to blame reality than ourselves.

From the letter of an ex-patient, written fifteen years after conclusion of his analysis; the gentleman adds that in the above formulation he has put into writing an oral statement of mine communicated to him during his treatment. Irrespective of its authorship, the formulation seems to me correct.

13. HARD AS NAILS OR PUSHOVERS?

A woman with a long career as a golddigger once said to me ironically: "Make up your mind! Are golddiggers hard as nails or are they pushovers?"

The answer is, of course, that they are both. To comprehend this it is necessary to understand that they operate invariably on the "two-layer" system. *Unconsciously* golddiggers are desirous only of kicks, humiliation, pain: in short, they are masochistic *pushovers,* provided they are confronted with a stronger person. Then inner guilt, mobilized because of the craving for kicks, forces the creation of a more superficial, though also unconscious, defense. The latter *seems* to make them *hard as nails,* provided they come in contact with a *weaker* person.

This double craving for psychic masochism and (as a defense) pseudo aggression explains the cynicism of golddiggers. If one exposes them as golddiggers and upbraids them (as do their mates), they admit it and are even flattered, taking the accusation as a confirmation—though with a negative connotation—of what they would like to believe of themselves: that they are hard as nails.

Sometimes golddiggers have, as they believe, a sad and sentimental history: "Don't think I've been hard-boiled from the start. I just got that way after a terrible disappointment. . . ." The disappointment credited with the making of a golddigger regularly turns out to have been an unhappy love affair. What these people overlook or are ignorant of is that the tendency to choose the disappointing lover was already present *unconsciously,* the result of the repressed masochistic tendency. Thus reasons and results are conveniently confused.

The general connection between *love and money* is replete with contradictions and hypocrisy. It is naïve to deny that a connection does exist. A woman who marries only for money is considered a golddigger, a prostitute with a wedding ring. So far, there is agreement. The trouble starts with more normal marriages: the hypocrisy is stubbornly maintained that a normal woman is above monetary considerations. This is not true. There is nothing abnormal about taking reality factors into consideration *before* marriage. For a normal person, love is a prerequisite for marriage, true. But it is useless to pretend that other factors— the standard of living, the social setting—are negligible considerations. A girl is not a golddigger because she asks herself before marriage what the prospects are.

The same holds true for a man. A man who marries solely for money or connections is a neurotic. If he refuses to work, insists upon being supported indefinitely, he is a specific type of neurotic —a playboy. So far, again, agreement prevails. The question once more begins with the evaluation of reality factors—and no reasonable person can deny that money and connections have a very definite importance in our society. Considering the social and economic factors before marriage does not make a man mercenary. The idea that the sphere of love is too rarefied for any thought of money to enter into it is simply a fake. On the other hand, marriage is not a crusade and is not normally used for the expression of political credos, racial or religious dogmas or family conflicts. People who marry against, rather than for, are neurotics who misuse external obstacles for their masochistic purposes, camouflaging this aim with the convenient blind of rationalizations.

The same holds true of conflicts about money in marriage. The absurd world we happen to live in still clings to the illusive picture of the he-man husband supporting the baby who is his wife. This conception of marriage, though time-honored, is also time-ridden. Women are not babies; they are full-fledged human beings. And men are not so strong as they are forced to pretend to be; in fact, biologically and psychologically, woman is the stronger, man the weaker sex.[1]

Conflicts about money enter nearly every marriage, at least transitorily. The trouble is deeply embedded in the male psychology which gratuitously assumes that the wife is a parasite for whom the husband must work himself to death. The problem is so important, and at the same time so complicated, that a separate section of this book has been devoted to it (Part Nine, Chapter 25).

Money, conflicts, and reproaches centering about money frequently express in sexual relations conflicts pertaining to the pre-money age of infancy. An intelligent, pretty girl in the early twenties presented herself to me with this problem:

"I've been thinking about myself and the reproaches I get from my friend, but I can't arrive at a satisfactory answer to the problem. Perhaps you can provide a solution. I'm twenty-three, live alone and support myself on a $60-a-week salary as a dental as-

---

[1] For the deduction, see Chapter XII ("The Myth of the Superior Male") of author's *Divorce Won't Help*, Harper & Bros., N. Y., 1948.

sistant. I've had a few transitory affairs; they didn't amount to much. Why? I guess because I picked the wrong people. Anyhow, they just wanted to sleep with me, and I acceded—I wanted to find out what it was all about. It was fun in a way, but always a headache afterward. Then I met my present friend. He's forty-two, but looks much older, and is an industrial tycoon. I was swept off my feet; his assurance—which is backed up by great success—made me admire him tremendously. Sex with him is pleasant, but nothing to rave about. Perhaps it's my fault—I don't know. The point is that he makes crazy scenes, accusing me of being unfaithful and a golddigger. It's not true—still, it disturbs me. I've read enough psychological books to know what a neurosis is: a conflict, dating from childhood and not conscious any more, is shifted onto an innocent bystander. Is that correct?"

"It is. I'm surprised that you figured it out correctly."

"Well, it didn't help me. I told myself, don't be a dope, the guy doesn't mean *you*. But his reproaches stir up something in me, and I get unhappy and cry—and he takes that as proof that his suspicions are well founded."

"What did you deduce from the fact that an unjustified reproach disturbs you so much?"

"Unfortunately my cleverness only works against me. I told myself that if his reproaches find an echo in me it must be because they touch some hidden chord."

"Correct."

"But I have no idea what it is. I know I'm not unfaithful and not a golddigger. I know I only want a good time now and that some day I'll marry and be a good wife. Obviously, then, I should disregard his scenes—but I don't."

"What does your friend complain about, specifically?"

"I see him a few times a week at impossible times. He calls up and wants to see me immediately. Well, I work, and I can only get away from my office occasionally. If I don't leave at once, he reproaches me with being in love with my boss. If I do leave, he says I care nothing about working and that I want to be discharged and become a kept woman. What is a working girl to do when her friend always wants to see her at exactly 11 A.M., giving her five minutes' notice?"

"How does your friend explain his unreasonable desire for sex at these odd hours?"

"There is never an explanation, only the command: " 'I need you at eleven!' "

"How do you react?"

"I'm flattered and furious at the same time. I've even observed that I respond more fully following such a conflict."

"Have you thought of giving up your job?"

"Yes, but I dismissed the thought immediately. I don't want to be dependent on my friend—that would be hell."

"Does he suggest it?"

"Yes and no. He contradicts himself continually."

"What about his accusation that you're a golddigger?"

"I scrutinized myself as honestly as I could. I'm definitely not a golddigger. I never ask him for money—I don't *want* his money."

"Does he spend any on you?"

"He can't take me to restaurants or night clubs—he's too well known, and of course he's married. I see him in my little apartment. He insisted that I change some of the furniture. It seemed silly to me, though I didn't really care one way or the other. It's not my fault that a carpet or a table that looked perfectly all right to me made him see red. Anyway, he ordered some new pieces—and I can't say I care too much for his taste. Oh, and he bought me an expensive diamond watch for Christmas—it's so luxurious that I can't wear it, actually."

"Does he give you money?"

"A few times I've found a hundred-dollar bill in my purse. I returned the money, which only made him furious. If I don't take money he is angry, if I do and deposit it in the bank, he calls me a golddigger."

"Why do you stick to him?"

"That's what I can't figure out. I know how dreary life can be when you haven't too much money, and I do want to have a few gay years before I marry and settle down—but this man's behavior doesn't make things very gay, and I'll probably end by getting married sooner than I meant to."

"Whom do you want to marry?"

"Some nice guy on my own level socially and financially. There are a few who keep calling me up now, but I don't want to see them—I seem to prefer my boy friend's scenes."

"You know more than is generally learned just by reading psychiatric books. Why is that?"

The girl laughed. "So you didn't believe me? You're right. I once had a boy friend who was psychoanalyzed. He told me a great deal about the female unconscious."

"Have you figured out at least tentatively what it is that attracts you in your friend's scenes?"

"*You'll* say it's some repetition from childhood."

"Never mind what I might say. What did *you* figure out?"

"To tell you the truth, I almost believe it's what you would say it is. I've been thinking about the boys I consider eligible for marriage—all nice, clean, young lower-middle-class boys and all in love with me—and I decided tentatively on one. Then I shuddered, because I began to suspect that what made him attractive to me was a specific scene that ended with my deciding not to see him again. In his fury, he slapped me—and then, of course, apologized. Well, when I thought about him as a possible husband I couldn't help suspecting that I *want* a man who is strong and aggressive—not really aggressive, you know, but quarrelsome and full of reproaches. I'd read in your books that a man is at bottom a little boy—and I can confirm what you say about 'the hoax of the he-man.' But I'm attracted to the reproachful-aggressive type, even though I see through his babyishness."

"Quite clever. Did you figure out where you acquired your love of scenes, reproaches, and accusations?"

"I'm stuck there. My mother made such scenes, but I hated her."

"Only analysis could show you the reasons. You know that we don't work by giving unsupported intellectual interpretations, even if the real interconnection can be deduced in the first interview."

"Couldn't you make me the exception?"
"It wouldn't do you any good."

There is such a great general fear of falling, or having fallen, into the hands of a golddigger or a playboy that even tangentially related, or actually unrelated, problems disturb many people. The conflict is frequently aggravated by a moralistic attitude resulting in such questions as: "Has a wife the right to be supported by her husband, or does this make her a golddigger?" And: "My husband wants to take a sabbatical year from the university in order to finish his book; I would have to support him during that period. Does this make him a kept man?" And: "My husband constantly accuses me of being a golddigger because I fight his pathological miserliness. Is the accusation justified?"

All these and similar fully *unjustified* scruples prove what money neurotics can make out of simple and commonplace facts.

The question of immunity to golddiggers and playboys is unanswerable without taking into consideration a few basic facts: Every adult human being wishes to be loved exclusively "for himself." Everyone inwardly considers himself the most wonderful person in the world, hence worthy of love, tenderness, and admiration.

This infantile evaluation of self, confronted with "the cold accretion called world" and with real people, is in search of the ideal the self has built up—a search which is called "looking for a suitable partner."

All conscious good intentions are in vain: the choice of the ideal corresponds to the infantile stencil. And if that unconscious stencil includes the masochistic wish to be mistreated, a golddigger or a playboy, respectively, will be chosen. There exists psychologically *no* artificially induced "immunity" (induced, that is, by means of warning or advice). There exists only a *natural* immunity, which causes one intuitively to avoid these types: the normal man is automatically immune to the golddigger, the normal woman to the playboy. The victims of golddiggers and playboys are sick people. That sickness can be cured by psychoanalysis, as can the sickness of the golddiggers and playboys themselves. But these neurotics, suffering as they are from a specific type of money neurosis, seldom consult the psychiatrist, and then only when in *acute* trouble. Golddiggers and playboys may be called scavengers of money. Their tragic victims are equally seldom persuaded to mend their ways psychiatrically. One is reminded, when observing them, of a line in one of Strindberg's tragedies: "What a pity for man."

PART FIVE: THE MISER

*. . . and the blindest thoughtlessness of expend-
iture has not destroyed so many fortunes as the
calculating but insatiable lust of accumulation.*

CHARLES CALEB COLTON (1780–1832)

14. AVARICE HAS RUINED MORE MEN THAN PRODIGALITY

The miser believes that of his own free will he has
chosen a way of life, one which gives him pleasure.
Probably no miser, were he to read the following
statement (misers are, notoriously, not buyers of
books, or of anything else), would believe it for an
instant: *his way of life is forced upon him; he must
lead it.* He must live out the specific defense forced
upon him by his unconscious—he has no conscious
choice. Only secondarily does the miser make out
of his unconsciously forced way of life a virtue.

Despite his wealth, the outer world senses in the

miser a pitiful human being. Some instinctive sense in people makes them understand that once the amiable attitude live and let live is abandoned, suffering and psychic illness enter the human being. The miser himself does not understand this. He neither lives nor lets live. Of all money neurotics, he wears the tightest blinders.

Parents who give their children the aim of being successful (generally, though not always unadmittedly, the making and amassing of money) would do well to elaborate on the theme in this manner: "Be successful, but be sure and retain the ability to enjoy the fruits of your work." This is excellent advice for children. Unfortunately, it is useless for the neurotic adult. A neurosis is beyond good advice.

The miser is automatically deprived of all the emotions which give light and color to life: tender love, friendly human relationships. He gets instead a bundle of fears, compulsions, and obsessions, all centered about money. What the miser calls his pleasures are, in reality, desperate inner attempts to sugar-coat the misery of being a miser. These pseudo pleasures consist of imaginary outwittings of imaginary enemies: the miser creates the illusion that he is surrounded by people who want to take advantage of him. The relentless pressure of fantasied aggressions, all directed against the poor miser, mobilizes his psychic masochism and forces him to more and more desperate countermeasures: faster and faster the pseudo-aggressive inner defense mechanism works: visible in refusal after refusal of money to any and all, until, at last, the miser stands triumphant, alone with his hoard. And down at the bottom is the *real* miser, enjoying not his money (one cannot enjoy what one constantly fears to lose), but only the unconscious alibi of proving *temporarily* to his inner conscience that he is not passively masochistic but aggressive.

Imagine a small boy with a stick in his hand, haunted by his fear of entering a dark room. "You coward," his inner conscience accuses him. "You enjoy being scared." To which the boy replies with bravado: "Who's scared? This is what I like! I'll go in there and shake my stick at the devils hiding in the room! I'll show you!" Who really believes that the little boy enjoys entering the dark room? Who really believes that the miser (a little boy with his stick changed into a checkbook) enjoys his way of life? To live under the pressure of psychic masochism and to be constantly forced to furnish inner alibis represents a segment of Hell which Dante neglected to mention in his *Divina Commedia.*

The possession of money is undoubtedly an advantage in our society. Very few wealthy people, however, are healthy enough to enjoy that advantage. In the majority they are afflicted with an occupational disease which can be called "money neurosis, department miser" (*the neurotic misuse of the rational fact of possessing money*). The miser type of neurotic is characterized by the following signs:

1. Obsessional thinking about money; worship of inactive money: cash, mortgages, stocks, bonds, etc.

2. Compulsive accumulating of money and/or greedy holding of inherited money, combined with abnormal miserliness.

3. Subordination of everything to money.

4. Being haunted by fear of losing money by external events.

5. Inability to enjoy even the power which money gives, because of inner fear and insecurity.

6. Constant excitement and expressed indignation at the thought of "being taken advantage of," combined with pathological suspicion.

7. Deep unconscious masochistic passivity, constantly counteracted by unconscious feelings of guilt because of that passivity.

8. As unconscious alibi against the chronic accusation of the inner conscience, pertaining to that masochistic passivity, a pseudo-aggressive defense mechanism is created: the constant outsmarting of imaginary enemies in the form of refusals of money and, occasionally, cynical callousness.

The word miser is an absolute one; speak it or write it and instantly the mind envisions an *old* man or woman, generally emaciated, with suspicious eyes, hovering with loving gloating over a pile of gold pieces. This, of course, is the conditioned vision of legend and folklore. Unfortunately, in a psychiatric-psychoanalytic sense, the miser neurotic is not absolute. Far from it. In varying degrees (miserliness, niggardliness, stinginess, penuriousness) the illness runs the full gamut of every group of society.

A patient in analysis, describing her husband's attitude toward money, explained with great indignation: "My husband is a miser, and a show-off of the worst kind. Yesterday in a restaurant he tipped the waiter by throwing a quarter at him, shouting: 'Catch!' The waiter, I am glad to say, had the dignity not to be taken in by it; he allowed the quarter to fall to the floor, looked at my husband with great contempt and said, 'Catch it yourself, you seem to have experience with dogs!' The quarter was only five per cent of the bill. The throwing of the quarter was my husband's method of cheating the waiter out of the customary fifteen per cent tip. If my husband spends as much as a penny he wants admiration for his magnanimity. He would cheat anyone for any reason and kill himself to acquire a penny."

Another patient complained that every time she was invited to her wealthy uncle's for dinner she left the table hungry. "Only potatoes in various culinary disguises are served," the patient said. "If you are still hungry you may have a second helping of these. If you mention, ever so carefully, to my uncle that there are other foods besides potatoes he flies into a rage." (The patient solved her difficulty by eating a hearty meal before going to her uncle's house.)

"My father is so stingy," whimpered a young man in analysis, "that he refuses to help me financially, although he is wealthy and I am his only son. Whenever I ask for help, he simply says, 'Nothing succeeds like success' and promises to match every thousand dollars I earn with a thousand dollars of his own. What hypocrisy! I need money now, to start out in business with, not later when I am already successful!"

The cloak of saving is used to disguise the illness of the miser neurotic. Once a wealthy old woman was asked how to make breaded veal cutlets. She gave the whole recipe, then as if in afterthought added: "Of course, if *you* can afford it, an egg should be used." Another woman of means described to one of my patients, with great pride, the system by which she spends only a dime for a year's supply of matches: "I save the wooden kitchen matches and use them over and over when the flame is burning to light other gas jets." The friend said ironically that it sounded like a good idea, unless, of course, one burned one's fingers. To which the saving woman indignantly retorted: "Unless you're a spendthrift, you just don't burn your fingers!" The son of a wealthy mother sent her a Christmas greeting card. "It was a very lovely card," his mother told him, "but why did you spoil it by signing it? If you hadn't I could have used it for somebody else."

These and similar examples familiar to all merely confirm Montaigne's thesis: "In plain truth, it is not want, but rather abundance, that creates avarice." By now it is a banal observation that the majority of wealthy people, who, allegedly, "cannot afford it," live *below* their means and the majority of people of moderate income who really cannot afford it, live *above* their means.

It is interesting to note that the expression "I cannot afford it" is used by both types with completely different intonation. The really stingy person—who can but does not want to afford it— pronounces the dictum with coldness and determination, as if doing something aggressive and being triumphant about it. The person of moderate income—who wants to afford it but really cannot—states the same phrase with regret, sometimes with accusing anger, and sometimes, generally when he is older, with a matter-of-fact attitude.

There are innumerable jokes pertaining to the pathologic stinginess of the wealthy.[1] True, some of them represent the ironic revenge of the less fortunate (the wealthy person's own terminology). Some are built on exaggerations of observable facts. For

[1] The simple explanation that the indignation in refusing money is connected with *conscious* guilt stemming from the possessing of money is erroneous and misleading (in general, an unwarranted consoling assumption on the part of people without money). Concentration here is upon cases in which a heightened emotional reaction occurs where there is not the slightest reason for displaying indignation, and where, in like circumstances, a normal person would simply say "No."

instance, the international joke with a hundred variations and applied to every millionaire in every country: A millionaire visiting in a summer resort wakes up one morning with a toothache, the result of chronic neglect of his teeth. Of course he tries hot packs and cold packs, for he cannot afford the extravagance of journeying to the city to pay the enormous fee of the greedy dentist. But the pain persists and, after consoling himself with the thought that dental expenditures are deductible on his income tax return, the millionaire walks six miles to a distant village (where he hopes no one will recognize him and therefore take advantage of his position of wealth) and consults the local dentist. "How much," he asks, "would you charge for the simple, easy job of pulling this miserable tooth?" The local dentist names his fee—three dollars. "Three dollars!" says the aggrieved millionaire. "Tell you what—just loosen it for a dollar, and I'll finish the job."

The element of outsmarting predominates in this and similar stories. The wealthy protagonist always behaves as if a conspiracy of professional robbers were to be fought, and he—the poor victim—must rely solely on his wits and ingenuity, and never on his money.

The thrifty person suffers seemingly from an exaggerated sense of justice in money matters. One such, a wealthy patient, said: "My wife works; I work. We have a fifty-fifty arrangement with regard to money. And it makes me furious when my wife takes advantage of our arrangement. For instance, as we are both working, neither of us is home for lunch. But she makes sandwiches out of the left-overs from dinner and takes them to her office; that's her lunch. She doesn't contribute anything to my lunch—why should I contribute fifty per cent to hers?" To my mild observation that the value of his wife's sandwiches, on a fifty-per-cent arrangement, might come to as much as ten cents, the patient answered indignantly: "A matter of principle is involved, if you please!"

What the man did not see was his misusing of the matter of ten cents for the warding off of old infantile injustice patterns, resulting in fear and, of course, the defense mechanism of being taken advantage of. Surely, a matter of principle was involved: that of the infantile fantasy of being unjustly treated. Only when confronted with a minute description of his own unconscious mechanism in analysis did the masochistic substructure—the true basis for his avowed principles—become clear to him. Nevertheless, his wife believed him to be pathologically stingy and used the lunch argument extensively to prove her diagnosis.

There exists a classical argument adduced by all people living by the principle "It is smart to be thrifty; one gets rich by saving pennies." Nothing could be further from real experience (all bank and insurance advertisements to the contrary). Still, the stated principle itself is interesting. It not only represents a convenient blind for miserliness but it also points to an additional emotional factor in stinginess. Saving pennies by the very act of not spending pennies proves the overestimation of pennies per se. Now, there is only *one* situation in life in which pennies, nickels, and dimes were of prime importance, and that situation is early childhood. Many a millionaire parts much more readily with one-hundred-dollar bills than he does with his dimes. And there's a reason for this: in the *pre*conscious, the penny, the nickel, and the dime have the emotional value of sweets, chewing gum, and ice-cream sodas. *Un*consciously, the coins have the emotional value of money stolen from mother's purse—the whole infantile pseudo-aggressive defensive conflict in miniature.

The reverse side of the *"coin of stinginess"* carries an invisible inscription: *"inability to enjoy leisure and luxury."*

How can anyone enjoy himself when he is constantly thinking about the amount of money he is about to spend? Under favorable conditions, money is a means to an end. The moment it becomes an end per se, the fun and pleasure it is supposed to provide evaporate.

A patient once described to me the following scene. During World War I he was stationed in a village where meat was very scarce. He was invited to dinner by a well-to-do family. Like a miracle, a roast of meat appeared on the dinner table. The guest and the entire family expressed their delight and pleasure at so rare a happening, with one exception, the hostess. She was too busy watching, with a strange intensity, her husband carve; her lips seemed to count the slices as they fell from the carving knife. Once the portions were passed, she tried to shift her intense glance from one to another, and as the company cut and raised pieces of meat to their mouths, she would exclaim, the words rushing out as if by themselves: "You are now consuming ten francs' worth of meat." The price varied with her gauging of the weight of each forkful. There was no emphasis on the rarity of what was being consumed, only on its price. My patient commented that he had never seen an unhappier-looking person; the woman seemed the victim of some strange anguish. What's more, he said, she was so busy watching and counting that she, herself, forgot to eat.

Recently, a wealthy patient told me of a conflict with his wife. They had decided on Cape Cod for a vacation, but he procrastinated so long that the reservation his wife had made for a cottage (he believed it too expensive) was lost. As there were no more cottages in this section, the best the wife could do was to reserve rooms at the local inn at the rate of $45 per week American plan. My patient's immediate reaction was "too expensive." His wife, however, pointed out that the price was very reasonable, so much so that she suspected the food at the inn would be of the poorest quality. She imparted her suspicions to her husband, consoling him with the thought that they would not be bound to eat at the inn every day, that there were many good restaurants close to it. At this the husband became infuriated, stating that their bill at the inn would be exactly the same whether they took the meals or not. He worked himself into a fury about something which had still to happen, and finally shouted: "I hate nothing more than to pay twice for the same thing!" Knowing the gentleman quite well, I suspect that even if the sinful waste of going out for an occasional good meal should not occur (and he will see that it does not), the mere possibility that it might happen will be enough to spoil the poor man's summer.

There is a general impression that puritanic-spartanic ideas are involved in these and similar irrational modes of behavior, or that a neurotically severe inner conscience objects to any luxury and leisure. But as far as I could observe clinically, this is a mirage—pure neurotic stinginess is at the bottom of the cycle. For instance, a patient, a physician with a large income, made his life miserable by his pathological approach to money. He was forever eating his heart out, felt himself constantly being taken advantage of, and was near a heart attack each time he felt unjustly treated. The objective substratum of all these emotions was always the same: dollars and cents. External circumstances forced him to take a vacation (left to himself he would gladly have killed himself with overwork). But a vacation would cost money. To surmount this, to him, insurmountable fact, he, a comparatively wealthy man, accepted the position of physician in a camp; he would have to work and the accommodations would be far from luxurious, but he would receive his room and board free and the idea of saving money was just too alluring to resist. For the first few days he felt happy and superior, then he learned about another camp which not only gave its physician free room and board but a small salary to boot. Almost at once my patient had one of his typical severe conflicts, became morose, ill; the conflict, as he stated it, pertained to the fact that he was not getting a small salary along with his room and board.

On the surface his conflict seemed to be about money, but what was really its basis was the fact that he felt he had been outsmarted. Once this had happened, the bogeyman of the nursery was once more on the march. The moment the miser cannot present to his inner conscience the pseudo defense of pseudo aggression (outsmarting the other fellow), he feels, under pressure of his inner guilt (because of his passivity), depressed and unhappy. As we already know, this inner conflict is then secondarily shifted to dollars and cents.

Before leaving the miser and going on to his opposite, the spendthrift, we would like to make the observation that a person suffering from money neurosis (department miser) is frequently incurable for the following three reasons:

First, he has not the slightest notion that he is ill, and therefore never enters treatment because of what is popularly called money madness. This part of his neurosis is discovered accidentally after he (or she) comes into psychiatric treatment because of depression, boredom, dissatisfaction, marital conflict, or some other neurotic conflicts such as impotence or frigidity. In some twenty years of psychiatric-psychoanalytical practice I cannot recall *one* individual entering treatment with the complaint: "My approach to money is peculiar."

Second, the neurotic approach to money has the approval and social backing[2] of the wealthy segment of our society and is therefore under *no external pressure.* There are very few wealthy people with a normal approach to money. Hence, where would external pressure generate from? Imagine a society in which impotence has social backing, a society in which a person could take social pride in impotence. In such a society, you may be sure, very few people would seek treatment because of that neurotic symptom specifically.[3]

Third, the miser type of money neurosis is genetically a deep-seated neurosis; it reaches the most complicated level possible in neurotic regression. Although today it is possible to cure this form of neurosis,[4] the complete lack of understanding on the patient's

[2]In all probability an old joke illuminates the phrase "social backing" in a better fashion than any sociological work: a stranger, visiting a small New England town, watched a man, obviously an old resident, walk down the main street. No one greeted him; no one returned his greetings. He was completely ostracized. The stranger, upon asking what horrible crime the man had committed, was informed that he offended moral principles: he touched the actual .interest from his capital, instead of living on the interest earned by the interest of said capital.

[3]On the other hand, the importance of external factors ("social backing") should not be exaggerated. Neurotics fight their *intrapsychic* battles, using as alibis external factors. The inner conscience (Super-Ego) is by no means a photographic copy of reality, nor a simple summation of external taboos. For elaboration see *The Battle of Conscience,* loc. cit.

[4]Readers with a smattering of analytic knowledge may be surprised that miserliness is not put on an "anal" basis. Freud found forty years ago that obsessional and compulsive neurotics frequently show this triad in their personality make-up: they are hypermeticulous, stingy, and stubborn. Ferenczi elaborated in 1914 on this theme in his well-known study on "Ontogenesis

part that a neurosis is involved, combined with social backing, explains why the cure of the clinical entity miserliness (in the larger framework of money neurosis) is the exception rather than the rule.

---

of Interest in Money." Róheim adduced anthropologic material ("Holy Money in Melanesia," *Internationale Zeitschrift f. Psychoanalyse*, 1923), connecting tentatively anal and oral mechanisms, although the underlying concept of orality, used in his deliberations, was identical with the wish "to get" and resultant aggression. My own investigations showed that a precise differentiation is necessary between the *historic-genetic* concept of orality, observable in the baby, where orality really means the wish to get, and the *clinical picture* in adult neurotics, where the original desire "to get" underwent masochistic elaboration. Hence the adult, orally regressed neurotic unconsciously does not wish to get, but to be refused. For theoretical discussion, see *The Basic Neurosis*, loc. cit.

Money is a good servant but a dangerous master.

DOMINIQUE BOUHOURS

15. TEACH YOUR DOLLAR TO HAVE MORE CENTS

The spendthrift is a neurotic carved out of the same wood as the miser. He starts out with the same inner conflict in infancy: masochistic attachment to the mother, and later to the father. This produces unconscious feelings of guilt, similar to those of the future miser. In other words, step one and step two are identical in both the future miser and the future spendthrift. At that point, the congruity ends. The third step (the alibi, the unconscious defense mechanism) is totally different. Whereas the miser uses pseudo aggression in the form of refusing money to others, the spendthrift applies an unconscious mechanism called magic gesture.

A magic gesture denotes an unconscious dramatization of the thought: "I shall show you, bad Mother and Father, how I really wanted to be treated—with kindliness and generosity." It is important to understand that the pseudo wish is already a defense and does *not* correspond at all to the dynamically decisive wish of the future spendthrift: he is already stabilized on the rejection level. What he is really after is psychic masochism. He achieves that goal by *depriving himself of money*.

To exemplify this point, here are two clinical cases:

The son of a wealthy mother was in constant conflict with her because of his reckless spending. In analysis he defended his actions with the statement that his strange indecision, and not he, was responsible for his difficulties. As proof he produced the following incidents. Wishing to order a few shirts, he went to an expensive shop where he saw hundreds of samples. Without hesitation and with great definiteness he narrowed down the range of choice to about thirty samples. Although he could thus readily separate the shirts he liked from those he considered in bad taste, he was totally incapable of narrowing the choice still further, and as there was no way out of his indecision he ordered all thirty shirts. On still another occasion he went to a bookstore in order to buy *one* recently published book. The salesman showed him, along with the book he had come to purchase, several dozen publications which had appeared within recent weeks. The patient rejected a number on the ground that they did not interest him. Still, fifteen books remained on the counter before him. The patient, unable to come to a decision, bought all fifteen.

From the history of this patient one learned that his mother had six children, and of the six she preferred some and neglected others. One of the neglected, in his own estimation, was the patient, who felt that he had been discriminated against. Without being conscious of it, he used his extravagance and indecision to act out a magic gesture, the unconscious meaning of which was the tearful accusation: "You, Mother, have discriminated against some of your children; you played favorites. I, however, cannot even choose between indifferent objects (shirts, books, etc.). How much less would I be capable of doing so among my own children!" Pathetic plea for a little kindness though it seems, it was but a covering cloak for the masochistic wish to suffer and to perpetuate his suffering.

A wealthy patient told me of an incident from her troubled life. Some years earlier she was, as usual, temporarily broke because of her own extravagance. Her family threatened her with serious steps. At the time she was stranded in Monte Carlo. Suddenly, and to her complete surprise, she began to win at the tables. At the moment of cashing in her chips she was approached by a casual acquaintance who told her a hard-luck story and asked for a loan of one hundred thousand francs. Without hesitation my patient loaned the acquaintance the amount requested, although at that moment her winnings, all the money she had in the world, came to exactly one hundred thousand francs. Furthermore, there was apparently no chance of getting any more funds from her embittered family. She made no attempt to ascertain the truth of the borrower's story; she asked for no receipt; nor did she inquire into the background of a woman she scarcely knew. She just gave her the hundred thousand francs. From that moment on, her luck changed. Since now she had to win in order to live, she lost and lost.

Many years after the incident (in analysis) it became clear that her extravagance was based upon a magic gesture.[1] Unconsciously, she expressed in her conduct: "My cruel family lets me starve. I, however, am charitable, even to a stranger. Moreover, the bad mother [Monte Carlo Casino] takes away everything from me and, after thus robbing me, allows me to starve." Needless to say, the casual acquaintance never repaid the loan. My patient did not even resent this; the unconscious thought being: "What can you expect from the bad mother?"

Analytically, we have ample experience with spendthrifts: the exasperated families of these neurotics, in their desperation, often send them into treatment. In my experience, the uncon-

[1]For details see Part Nine, " 'Gift-Touchy' Money Neurotics."

scious reason for the behavior of spendthrifts is always a magic gesture.

The usurer and the loan shark are necessary to the spendthrift. With one foot always in the lawyer's office and the other in prison, the rationalizations of these people vary to a great extent. This does not make the usurer, least engaging of all money neurotics, any more appetizing a specimen. Very few human beings can attain his utter cynicism and hypocrisy. In Balzac's *Gobseck*, there may be found a passage in which the usurer's friend asks him why he lends him money only at an exorbitant rate of interest, and the usurer answers:

I wanted to save you the feeling of gratitude, my friend, giving you the right to assume that you don't owe me anything. Therefore, we still are good friends.

The passion for money as encountered in the usurer is insatiable, as is his inability to enjoy his money. The ironical remark of the French statesman, Duc de Choiseul, belongs here: "If you see a man in Geneva jump from his window, follow him; there is at least six per cent to earn." Geneva seems to have many substitutes in this world.

There are two types of neurotics, both of which are slightly ridiculous or, more precisely, tragicomic, whose attitudes toward money are contradictory.
The "second-generation type."
This type of neurotic dresses on principle in a shabby fashion (the leading idiosyncrasy is in the matter of dress; one often mistakes the millionaire for the beggar). He lives frugally, watching his necessary expenses with great care. Careful, cautious, he is proud of his meager way of life and looks with contempt upon the *nouveau riche*. He constantly uses the phrase "I can't afford it." He is pathologically suspicious lest someone take advantage of him. He worships the very act of refraining from spending money. His fear mounts close to panic at the thought of losing his money. He constantly claims that both government expendi-

tures and taxes are ruinous (March is his worst month). His pride is concentrated in the conviction that only a fool spends money without long deliberation (he, of course, thank God, is not such a fool). In his view, pleasure in life consists in disguising the fact of possession of money of looking askance at the extravagances of spendthrifts (to him, practically the whole world), and, finally, of warding off the repeated, never-ceasing attempts of rascals desirous of exploiting him. He invariably offers forty to fifty per cent of any stated purchase price. He is a firm believer in the act of impressing and intimidating others with the sheer weight of the *reputation* of possessing money. The moment anyone allows himself to be intimidated or impressed by his money, he despises that person as a nonentity and, given the opportunity, squeezes him mercilessly.

The only way in which one can hold one's own with this type of neurotic is to call his bluff, thus showing him that you are *not* impressed. But, to call his bluff with a bluff of your own will prove of no avail; it is useless to fake or pretend with him, for, like a child, he has a very acute sense of whether or not people actually see through him.

The "parvenu type."

This type lives in constant fear that no one will believe he is well off. The phrase "I cannot afford it" never comes to his lips. He is a flashy dresser, buys only the very latest, overpays, overtips. He looks down upon, really despises, the unsuccessful person, taking considerable pleasure in poking fun at him. In general, he comes from the wrong side of the railroad tracks, but always attempts to disguise the fact (exceptions being the overstressing of the self-made attitude). His ambitions are conventional; he is a social climber and a snob. Easily impressed, especially by the static wealth of the second-generation type, he admires money and has to prove constantly, to himself and others, that he possesses it and can afford to spend it. Inwardly he is as stingy as the second-generation type; however, his inner necessity of proving that he is financially a big shot overshadows his greed.

The parvenu type is a free spender for display purposes in

public; in private, at home, we often find him to be a merciless miser. If you are not impressed by his public display, the bubble of pretense collapses almost immediately and the primitive unadulterated personality comes to the fore.

Once I analyzed a man and his wife simultaneously; he came from the right side, she from the borderline of the wrong side of the tracks. He had inherited a great deal of money; she, in her profession, earned quite large sums. At one time, they received a worthless unframed painting as a gift from a stingy relative. The painful irony of the situation was the fact that they both felt the necessity of displaying the painting in their apartment (neither wished to insult the wealthy relative). But even more painful than this was the fact that they had to buy a frame for the worthless canvas. At the framer's the following scene took place. The dealer quoted them a price of twelve dollars. At the mention of the sum, the husband immediately told the dealer with great indignation that he could not afford to pay twelve dollars for a frame.

His wife, relating the incident to me in analysis, said: "I nearly died of shame. I have known this dealer for years. He respects me for my social position. Why must my husband make a show of our financial circumstances in front of him?"

Here, in a nutshell, we see the differing approach to the phrase: "I cannot afford it." He, being wealthy from early childhood on, simply meant: "I can, of course, afford it, but I don't want to be made a sucker." She, in her parvenu manner, was shamed by his use of the phrase and could think of it only as an admission of poverty to the dealer. In fact, I am sure that under no circumstances would the phrase "I cannot afford it" ever come from her lips.

The pathological greed of the wealthy neurotic is matched only by his pathologic suspicion that everyone wants to take advantage of him. Here is a classical example:

A patient informed me that a wealthy acquaintance of hers, a young sculptor, had asked her for my name and address. "He is very strange," the patient said. "He collects the names of psychiatrists from all his friends. I don't know what he intends to do with them; he can't consult all the psychiatrists, especially as he doesn't differentiate among schools of psychiatry." Some weeks later, the collector of psychiatric names called up and asked for three appointments.

"Why exactly three?" I asked him.

"Well, I have to make a diagnosis," was the unperturbed reply.

"Do you mean it will take three appointments for me to make my diagnosis of your case?"

"You misunderstand. It will take *me* three appointments to make *my* diagnosis as to whether or not you are the right analyst for me."

The appointments were arranged. The young man appeared for the first one, carrying a large trunklike suitcase containing photographs. He explained that he needed these photographs to exemplify his life history. I asked him: "But why are *three* appointments necessary, since you are just here, as you say, to make a diagnosis? If you are so sure you can make one, why not in one appointment?"

My irony was lost on the young man, who answered seriously: "I have to tell you my life history, and that will take three hours." Then, sensing a certain skepticism in me, he said: "You seem to doubt my ability to make a correct diagnosis among the ten psychiatrists whose names I've collected and whom I have been consulting during the past few weeks. You see, I'm shopping around. You're the eighth on my list."

I answered that this shopping around would undoubtedly produce results. For instance, his bank account would diminish. He would obtain a knowledge of the interiors of offices, and would have an opportunity to study accents, tone of voice, suits, brands of cigars and other important human characteristics. "You will find out many things of the same kind; the one thing you will *not* learn is whether or not the object of your investigation is a good analyst."

To this the patient replied with perfect confidence: "You are mistaken."

"What do you want me to do during your test?" was the last question I ventured.

"Nothing. You just listen," was the young man's answer, clearly indicating that he considered my questions a senseless waste of time.

He began to tell me the external facts of his life, starting with birth, and illustrating important facts pictorially. He had no photographs of his birth, but he had some of the house in which the memorable event took place, of his mother at that period, and so on. He had traveled a good deal, and many of the pictures pertained to that part of his life. He showed me also a photo depicting his first artistic endeavor, a church built out of a child's blocks. This review of photographs went on throughout three appointments. In accordance with the patient's request, I did not utter a single word.

At the end of the third appointment he said: "As I told you, you're the eighth on my list. I have to consult two more of your colleagues. That will take a week—or six days, to be exact. At the end of next week I shall inform you of my decision, should the choice fall on you."

"One moment, please," I interrupted. "Your appointment has ended and I would like to make two remarks on my own time. First, you are playing some neurotic game which I don't pretend to understand. It is obvious that you derive some pleasure from playing off these ten people against one another. Otherwise you could consult them all without any of them knowing about the others. Second, since you must disappoint nine of them by choosing only one, let me say that you seem to have an exaggerated idea of the amount of pleasure or unhappiness you will bestow by accepting or rejecting us. True, we depend on our patients, but not on any *one* patient."

The young man looked slightly taken aback, but murmured again: "You are mistaken," and took his leave. A week later he informed me that he had decided to start treatment with me. I asked for the reasons for his decision.

"As you suspected," said the young man, smiling proudly, "I showed those hundred of photographs for a specific purpose. *One* of them constituted my test; everything else was camouflage. We wealthy people must constantly guard against individuals who flatter us because of our money. I decided that every colleague of yours who made a complimentary remark about my first attempt at artistic creation was automatically out. You were the only person who returned the church photograph without a flattering remark. Therefore you passed my test. . . ."

16. MONEY IS NOT REQUIRED
TO BUY ONE NECESSITY OF THE SOUL[1]

The counterpart of the admirer of money is the despiser of that commodity. Both are neurotics. The honest despiser of money (the insincere variety is just as often encountered) operates on an idealistic level from which one finds it difficult to dispossess him: the everyday world is greatly impressed by the despiser of that which they hold most dear. True, the primitive and avid type of "money-mad" person is not an engaging type. His disregard for anything not measurable in dollars and cents is repelling. But,

[1]Thoreau.

despite all this, it does not necessarily follow that the reactive type promoting the opposite attitude is automatically right. The despiser of money has his unconscious reasons too. These can be observed clinically.

Mr. A., an attorney, entered treatment because of what he called a nervous breakdown. He was forty-three years of age and had lived all his life with his mother, and, allegedly because he had to take care of her, had never married. A few months before his collapse his mother had died. In analysis he stated that he was incapable of working, that he had lost all interest in earning a living. Asked what his objections to making money were, he answered, "Whether you're a poor man or a millionaire, you can eat only one steak for dinner." Asked how he intended to finance even the simplest of steak dinners, he retorted that, as his tastes were very simple, he had enough money to last him for some time. He said, "When I look at my wealthy clients and see their mad drive for money, I doubt if the whole game is worth the candle." Upon being questioned as to whether his rejection of money was newly acquired or a phenomenon of long standing, he replied that it was of many years' duration. "As long as my mother lived, I had to make money in order to support her comfortably. Now everything is changed."

To which I inquired: "What about your girl? Don't you need money for her?"

"Who cares about her," the patient said, "that golddigger!"

"But if she's a golddigger, why did you choose her as a friend?"

"That's a silly question. All women are out after money."

"Including your mother?"

"No. She was totally different. Sure, she expected a certain amount of comfort out of life, but then she was entitled to it."

"There are six brothers and sisters in your family. Some of them are well off. Why didn't they contribute to the support of their mother?"

"Because they're married and have families of their own."

Thus confusing reasons with results, this otherwise intelligent man had a rationalization for every action. Analysis of the patient revealed that his unconscious relationship with his mother was far more complex than he knew and therefore impossible for him to put into words. Although his descriptions of his mother were those of a kindly and devoted woman, they were complemented by the patient's intense feeling that she was some kind of a spider, enveloping him in her net. Very often he felt (as he later admitted) helpless fury at his mother's arrogant assumption that all her demands on his private life and spare time would be granted without question. Unconsciously he cultivated this latent rebellion (which, in her lifetime he had never voiced), because such a revolt furnished him with his favorite alibi against the reproach of his inner conscience, which constantly and justifiably accused him of enjoying his mother's tyranny. The patient had emerged from his early childhood with a deep masochistic attachment to his dominant mother: to be mistreated became his inner wish.

One of his techniques for being unjustly treated was forcing upon himself the necessity for earning more money than he would have needed for himself. And while so doing, he dwelt over and over again on his own modest needs. In this manner every hour of additional work he put in could be utilized as a reproach directed against his exploiting mother. That he unconsciously not only tolerated but directly created the entire situation became obvious very soon after the beginning of his analysis. Never had he protested the mother's expenses; never did he ask that his brothers or sisters contribute to her upkeep; and, last but far from least, never once did he insist on his own right to privacy, to an apartment of his own. Very soon I got the impression that all acts of displeasure derived from his connection with his mother were not only *not avoided* but were deliberately, though unconsciously, cultivated.

The patient's rejection of money had nothing whatever to do with money. Money was merely used as the external tool in his intrapsychic fight with his inner conscience, the latter rejecting his hidden masochistic pleasure gain.

Mr. B., at the time he consulted me, was an unsuccessful painter who seldom painted. He lived in the greatest poverty, despising money on ideological grounds. He was given to long and involved perorations about his soul. When asked the reason for his turning out so little work, he said accusingly, "What's the good of creating masterpieces? Either they're not appreciated, or, at best, they are bought by some wealthy ignoramus who displays them for the admiration of his drunken guests."

In analysis it turned out very soon that the real reason why the patient did not paint was because of a neurotic inhibition. Amusingly enough, the man had been sent into treatment by his wealthy uncle, not because of his antimoney complex or because he could not paint, but because of kleptomania. The uncle paid for the treatment, as he stated piously, as a tribute to his beloved dead sister (the real reason being that his nephew's kleptomania escapades reflected upon himself and were socially embarrassing). It could be proved in the patient's case that his despising of money was a complicated defense: instead of admitting to himself that he was incapable of earning money with his art because of his neurosis (he was so inhibited that he could no longer paint at all),[2] he preferred to despise money on principle, thus saving himself (at least consciously) the need of reproaching himself. However, he never failed to use money when ranting against his uncle: "Why should this stingy old fool be so furious about *my* kleptomania?"

Mr. C. was a musician, supported (on a small scale as he termed it) by his family. The truth of the matter was that the family made great sacrifices in order that he might study. In return, he did not study at all; he spent his time with his obsessions and compulsions. Asked what right he thought he had to cheat his family in this manner, he answered that he didn't believe in money, only in the higher things of life. This neurotic had a peculiar way of coping with his guilt, one which enabled him at the same time to achieve a queer masochistic pleasure. His family lived abroad. Every month they would send him his allowance check. The patient would spend his entire allowance the first week of the month. For the remaining three weeks he starved himself. In this way, month after month, he proved to himself how cruelly his family treated him: they let him starve.

[2]See *The Writer and Psychoanalysis*.

By this trick, the patient acted out what may be called a negative magic gesture. He dramatized the unconscious thought: "I shall show you by my behavior how I don't want to be treated." In other words, he acted out superficially an accusing gesture, making himself the victim. What he did not even suspect (as he ironically claimed, "even unconsciously") was that he liked this imaginary mistreatment, as was visible in the fact that he himself constructed the situation of starvation.

Love is an ocean of emotions, entirely surrounded by expenses.

LORD DEWAR

17. A MONEY MATCH IS ALWAYS A MISTAKE[1]

There are neurotics who admire money to such an extent that even the most private affair in life—marriage—becomes a hunting ground for it (or, at the very least, a reassurance against having to work for a living). To the normal individual the very idea of selling his emotional and sexual life for money is absurd and not worthy of a moment's serious consideration. As the normal person is the last to deny the importance of money in our society, he is also

[1]George Norman Douglas, Chapter 11 of *South Wind*, Dodd, Mead & Company, 1925.

the last to consider the fact that if either partner of a marriage has money it is a disadvantage. But the normal person's choice of mate is not made solely because of money; it can only be an additional soothing factor. *To marry exclusively for money is a certain sign of emotional abnormality.*

We have already seen in the golddigger and playboy the pitfalls of one type of money match. This *second type* denotes something quite different from the one previously described. It is so difficult to classify that I was a long time in giving it a name, but it does have definite and precise characterizations: two independently wealthy individuals marry each other, not because of love or any other emotional involvement, but for *social convenience.* Wealth is the prerequisite to marriage for one reason and one reason only: *to avoid the danger of supporting the mate.* These are wealthy men who consider the custom of supporting a wife a barbaric institution. There are wealthy women who are in mortal terror of falling into the hands of a fortune hunter. If it were not so clumsy a name, we might call this type of neurotic marriage the *"money-marries-money"* type. For the impersonal element in this nomenclature corresponds to the inner predilection and only love of these people—money.

In analyzing neurotics of this type, one finds with great regularity a complete inability to love tenderly. To the colorblind person, lack of colors or an impossible combination of colors does not seem queer. In like fashion, to the cold fish (as one patient of this type quite correctly characterized himself) the lack of emotions is nothing to worry about.

A patient, a man of forty, stated: "You asked me, Doctor, why I married my wife. Your implication being, I suppose, that I married because of what people call love. I consider your question senseless. No hard feelings, Doctor, but I'm surprised that you should fall for all that romantic twaddle. Love is an emotion invented by people who capitalize on it. Writers and poets, I mean. In real life things are different. Sure, from time to time you want to sleep with a woman, but even the sexual element, in my opinion, is highly overrated. But there is a strong social pressure exerted—a man has to marry, otherwise he is considered a fairy. So I married—a reasonable and wealthy girl. When I looked her over as a prospective wife, I asked myself one question: Assuming she were a prostitute, would I sleep with her? Since I could answer that question in the affirmative, I married her. Both of us are financially independent. Both of us are careful with our money. She has good money sense, thank God. But, Doctor, if you are trying to make some connection between my marriage and the reason I consulted you, the fact that I was dissatisfied with life in general, you'll be making a big mistake. . . ."

Another patient, a man of thirty-eight, explained his philosophy of marriage as follows: "The idea of supporting a woman in marriage seems to me a relic of barbaric times. I want to marry in order to improve my situation, not to worsen it. My future wife must support herself, either with inherited money or by income. I'm tired of spending money for dinners and night clubs on different girls who only want to take you for a sucker. . . ."

A man of thirty consulted me because of alcoholic addiction; when speaking of his father, he revealed his attitude toward marriage: "I was twenty when my father, on his deathbed, gave me this advice. First: Never change your stockbroker; second: Drink, but don't become a drunkard; third: Never marry for love, or marry a woman who has less money than you. I followed my father's advice, with the exception of the drinking, and it's about the drinking I need your help. But my poor father knew what he was talking about, all right. He married for love, and the result was that his wife supported her lovers on *his* money. He divorced her, and became embroiled in one scandal after another. Then he lost some money speculating. He started to drink to excess. Poor Father, he wasn't a good prophet after all. I'm just drinking myself to death. I'm immune to love. I have an arrangement with a nice girl. I'm going to marry her, I hope before we both have delirium tremens. We are both independent financially. We'll get around to marrying when she gets tired of sleeping around with any playboy on the loose. I believe sex plays a greater part in a woman's life than in a man's, all statements to the contrary notwithstanding. Why not let the girl have all her silly affairs before marriage? Look what happened to my father, who did it the other way round. In my opinion my future wife doesn't really enjoy sex at all. She seems frigid to me. So, all right, let her make herself absurd: let her learn her lesson. . . ."

One after another, these neurotics of the "money-marries-money" type voice their philosophy of love and marriage, always on the same note, a flat, dull, thwarted note.

And the women of the "money-marries-money" variety, what of them?

A patient, a wealthy woman of thirty-three, suffering from severe neurotic headaches, which, as she stated, made her life a veritable hell, answered my question about her marital status with complete cynicism: "I know what you mean, Doctor: you just asked in a roundabout fashion whether I am sexually normal. And, believe me, I was just waiting for it. Doctor, it gives me a great pleasure to give my honest opinion to a scientist who believes in normalcy. You and your books on frigidity in women! My dear Doctor, I hope you don't really believe this trash you are promoting, because if you do, I must consider you terribly naïve. Or maybe you've been taken in by a clever but cheating woman. *Orgasm in women does not exist!* You can like it or hate it, but this is—to quote your own favorite phrase—a clinical fact. The only thing a woman can get out of sex is distaste to a greater or lesser degree. Knowing this, I looked for the only two real things a clever and wealthy woman can achieve in marriage: money and *the assurance of not being forced to support a husband.* I don't want to be kissed out or kicked out of my money. If I have a neurosis, it manifests itself not in frigidity but in my wrong evaluation of the financial chances of my husbands. I have been married four times. My first two husbands each went broke a short time after we were married. Instead of supporting them, I sensibly divorced them. My third husband also went broke, but at least he had the decency to commit suicide. My fourth and present husband is the son of a very wealthy father—I have to manage him."

At one time a woman of thirty-five consulted me because of frigidity. She was familiar with my opinion that there is nothing wrong with marriage, but that there is something very wrong with

the *neurotic* participants in marriage. With this opinion she dis-
agreed heartily. "How on earth can you write such out-and-out
nonsense?" she asked. "Everything is wrong with marriage. Take
my experience as example. We were a rich family. Then, suddenly, in 1929, our money was gone. I was twenty, and to help
my family financially I married a man twelve years older than
myself. I had to endure his body and his reproaches and, on top
of it all, the ingratitude of my own family. Whatever I did for
them was not enough; they are a bunch of true parasites. For the
first few years I had the consoling fantasy of sacrificing myself
for my family; they cured that themselves, quick. Then I became skeptical of whether I am capable of what is so poetically
called love. I started a series of affairs. Each was a complete
fiasco. My husband died and left me his fortune. I consoled myself with the money. Now I want to marry again, but he has to
be a wealthy man. Not that I need his money. I just don't want to
support a husband. It's not easy, you know, for a rich widow
surrounded by playboys. But I found an eligible man. Then a
malicious girl friend of mine gave me a book of yours. You claim
that frigidity can be cured by analysis. Well? Do you suggest
that I start treatment before or after marrying my fiancé?"

"Do you love him?" I asked her.

"Stop that nonsense!"

"I think, then, you had better wait. Perhaps after becoming a
normal human being, you may approach the whole question in a
different fashion."

"I don't believe you. But why not give it a try—it's the popular modern fairy tale. And I can afford it."

"Please," I said. "Why do you keep on trying to fool yourself
about your motives?"

"Meaning exactly what?"

"Just a minute ago you stated that the assurance with which
some of my colleagues and I claim that frigidity can be cured
made you skeptical toward your own skepticism about sexual
enjoyment. And now you've said that only your wealth pushes
you into an analytical experiment, which you refer to as a fairy
story. It can't be both. And it's my guess that it's neither."

"Well, I am unsure of everything—if that's what you wish to hear."

"I have no wishes in this matter."

"You're not going to sit there and tell me that there's more to my coming here than—well, my sex problem?"

"I'm not going to tell you anything. But there is more to it, as you shall find out once you're in treatment."

"What more can there be?"

"Your whole inner guilt."

"I don't know what you're talking about."

"No, I don't suppose so, but you will find out."

Now, what is wrong with these men and women? On one point they are consistent. All of them deny that the emotion called love exists. On the medical plain there is consistency too. All are neurotics. The gentlemen found the thought of having to support a wife intolerable; the ladies wanted some assurance of not having to support a husband. All these pathological personalities seemed to have only one measuring rod: money. Having analyzed most of the cases quoted above, and many others of the same variety, I came to some definite conclusions. In cases such as these, money is *not* the original yardstick. It is the consoling "end thought" in a hopeless neurotic and therefore unconscious entanglement.

Neurotic men who cannot bear the thought of supporting wives are the victims of an early infantile conflict: instead of identifying themselves unconsciously with the *giving* mother, they become masochistically attached to their fantasied maternal *refusal.* To counteract the reproach of their inner conscience, which objects to "stabilization on the rejection level," they promote a violent and pseudo-aggressive defense mechanism, the one purpose of which is—refusal. Later, when they are older, that defensive refusal leads to refusal in monetary matters. These neurotics are far less smart in a realistic fashion than they think they are. They pay for the inner defense with the inability to enjoy tender and sensual emotions. A bad business deal. For, in due time, even their purely mechanical, lustless potency fails them.

Women of the "money-marries-money" variety are victims of the identical conflict with an additional variation: they are all frigid. From this dilemma they attempt to rescue themselves by denying the very possibility of normal sexual feelings.

Fortunately, the combination of tender and sensual emotions popularly called love does exist, and it can be restored even in these severe neurotics.

*How inexpressive is the meanness of being a hypo-
crite . . .*

VOLTAIRE, *A Philosophical Dictionary*

18. STRANGE, THAT BLOODSUCKERS LIKE TO MORALIZE[1]

The trappings of hypocrisy are often utilized by
money-greedy individuals in defense of their conscious aims. It is quite within the bounds of reason
that, once having gained his objective, such an individual might quite bluntly state: "I had the chance
of making the most out of a situation. I did so."
Strangely enough, in our society, such a statement
is rarely made. There is always a quasi-moral reason adduced to explain the act: seemingly to convince the cheated victim that no injustice has been

[1]Erich Maria Remarque, *Arch of Triumph*, D. Appleton-Century, 1935.

done him and, quite frequently, that he should feel gratitude for having been taken advantage of. Many naïve persons attempt to explain hypocrisy by the statement that this attitude simply reflects a precautionary measure: after so overt an aggressive act, why should the cheater go out of his way to collect ill will? But the cheated person is seldom deceived by pious hypocrisy, rarely taking it at its face value. The victim feels it as a new attack on his intelligence, the adding of insult to injury. For all these reasons the hypocritical approach does not reflect rational facts. Nevertheless, hypocrisy persists. In fact, it is one of the most prevalent of surface maneuvers in our society. The reason for its persistence is this: *the act of hypocrisy is unconscious in origin and a neurotic sign.*

Hypocrisy is a mechanism which acts in the *unconscious* Ego. It expresses the result of an inner conflict and has in its origin no connection with the outer world victims of the hypocrite. The existence of the pattern of hypocrisy proves that a constant intrapsychic conflict between Ego and inner conscience (Super-Ego) does exist.[2] Both the Ego and the Super-Ego of the hypocrite are characterized by specific features. The Ego of the hypocrite, although weak, is both elastic and cunning, unable to renounce its high-pitched narcissism. The Super-Ego of the hypocrite was originally built also according to patterns of educators who tyrannically insisted on acceptance of their rules, aggressively enforcing these without regard to whether acceptance was real or only lip service. In typical circumstances (weak Ego, aggressive Super-Ego) the result is submission of the Ego. In the case of the hypocrite exactly the opposite occurs: The Ego tricks the conscience on the basis of *pseudo submission.* In other words, it accepts all demands of the conscience only as a formality, accompanied by constant mockery of the stupid introjected educator who takes pseudo acceptance as a real one and lip service as real conviction. From that outsmarting of the Super-Ego the Ego derives a great deal of hidden narcissistic pleasure.

In the case of the hypocrite the unusual fact is that under the disguise of a victory of the Super-Ego a mockery of the Super-

[2]For elaboration see *The Battle of the Conscience.*

Ego takes place. The Super-Ego is made fun of in its own house, so to speak, thereby reversing the typical role of Ego and Super-Ego.[3]

In modern literature there is a classical scene in which money and hypocrisy walk hand in hand; it can be found in Remarque's *Arch of Triumph*. A well known Parisian physician, a Dr. Durant, employs the services of an unknown refugee surgeon, a Dr. Ravic, to perform "ghost operations." In the scene both doctors are dressed and ready for the operation, the patient already under anesthetic. Dr. Ravic, the refugee surgeon whose fee in such cases is a meager two hundred francs, is in desperate need of a larger sum and takes this opportune moment to demand a fee of two thousand francs. Dr. Durant, the hypocrite who is to receive ten thousand francs for an operation he will not perform, demurs. They argue back and forth, and finally Durant offers the refugee surgeon the sum of one thousand francs.

"Two thousand," Ravic corrected him.

Durant did not consent. He stroked his goatee. "Listen, Ravic," he said with warmth. "As a refugee who isn't allowed to practice——"

"I should not perform any operations for you," Ravic interrupted him calmly. Now he expected to hear the traditional comment that he ought to be grateful to be tolerated in the country.

But Durant forewent that. He could see that he wasn't getting anywhere and time pressed. "Two thousand," he said bitterly, as if each word were a banknote fluttering out of his throat. "I'll have to pay it out of my own pocket. I thought you would remember what I've done for you."

He waited. *Strange,* Ravic thought, *that bloodsuckers like to moralize. This old cheat with the rosette of the Legion of Honor in his buttonhole reproaches me for being exploited by him, instead of being ashamed. And he even believes it . . ."*[4]

This excellent description of Remarque's corresponds to clinical facts on hypocrisy. But the entire problem is not understand-

[3]For elaboration see Chapter 9, of *The Battle of the Conscience.*
[4]Italics are mine.

able without some knowledge of the inner structure of the unconscious part of the conscience. Here is a clinical example of neurotic hypocrisy; although negatively connected with money (the patient was treated free) it is classical in its dimensions.

Twenty-two years ago in the Vienna Psychoanalytic Clinic I made the following experiment: I was interested in finding out to what degree of human "stupidity" psychoanalysis could be effectively applied. Since in private practice we deal with persons with some degree of intelligence, I wanted to ascertain if people with a low I.Q. could, despite this handicap, be influenced analytically. With the help of one of the superiors in the clinic, I selected among two thousands patients on our waiting list a man who appeared to be mentally the most primitive, one who made his living by means of what even his wife called his low intelligence. The man was a peddler of soaps, and his customers bought his wares out of pity. On advice of a physician he wanted to be treated, without fee, because of erective impotence, threatening to commit suicide if his condition could not be changed. I felt that even he could be helped, provided the analyst took the trouble to explain, as far as the intellectual part went, the complicated phenomena of an hysteric impotence in simple childlike language. I was sure that in the affective (the unconscious level) there would not be the slightest difference between him and intelligent patients.

The patient entered analysis, behaved very submissively, but, as expected, started very soon to repeat in the transference situation his oedipal aggression toward his father, which was for him a defense mechanism against his deeper repressed passivity. By no means could he be brought to admit his inner aggression and resulting feeling of guilt. After a few months his sexual interest in his wife improved and, after the typical ebb and flow of success and failure, he performed normal intercourse one morning for the first time in his life. He did this at exactly 7:30 A.M. At 9 A.M. he came for his analytic appointment and was overenthusiastic about his success, wanted to kiss my hands, and cried with happiness. At exactly 2 P.M. of the same day he appeared without previous announcement in the office of my immediate superior in the clinic, the colleague with whom he had spoken in my presence before being definitely sent to me. There he complained about me. *He did not mention his successful intercourse,* but simply stated that he was wasting his time with me since no improvement was visible. My colleague told him that if he had resistances he should fight them out with me. The patient implored him not to mention the fact of his complaining to me. My colleague, of course, refused to do this; on the contrary, he asked him specifically to analyze the entire incident with me on the following day.

The next day the patient came for his appointment and began with the question: "Have you seen Dr. X. already?" My colleague had not informed me of the incident, considering it simply a typical acting out in resistance not worth mentioning, but the word "already" sounded suspicious to me and I asked the patient why I should have seen Dr. X. "Oh, only because you know him well," the patient answered. I insisted on some explanation, and slowly, almost word by word, I extracted from him the story of his actions on the day before. Once the incident was reconstructed, I asked him: "Why did you complain on the very same day that you had intercourse successfully for the first time in your life? And why did you not mention that fact to my colleague?" At this, the patient *smiled hypocritically* and informed me that he had some doubts of a general nature. "Is intercourse really so important?" was the tune he repeated. I reminded him that he had threatened to commit suicide if he could not achieve intercourse. Almost at once the patient changed his approach, cried, accused himself of hypocrisy and ingratitude, and begged me for some humiliating task in expiation. After that incident the analysis progressed normally. He was cured and discharged a few months later, and I was repeatedly invited by him to the ritual circumcisions of his sons who were produced regularly for a number of years.

What was the reason for the patient's queer behavior? That he repeated in transference his hatred of his father was clear. That he repeated that hatred in self-damaging conditions was also apparent, since his lies were so easily detected. That he masochistically did not want to be cured was visible too, since he assumed that I would dismiss him after his insolent act (that analysts do not react in such a manner in analysis he did not know). But all these facts are unimportant with regard to our problem: the explanation of hypocrisy.

I believe that we can observe in this case *in statu nascendi* the re-enactment of the genesis of the hypocritical reaction. The patient repeated in the transference the father-son relation. His father was a severe disciplinarian; he preached authority, especially the orthodox Jewish one. The patient acquired toward him an attitude of deep submission with a defense counterraction, pseudo aggression. Both he repeated with me, despite the fact that I behaved very differently from his father. He simply projected the old pattern upon me. Where his father was authoritative I was friendly, explaining, trying to make him co-operate without coercion. For a long time the discrepancy in his behavior was explained to him without effect. His attitude was that of submissive nonacceptance of interpretations. He was so submissive that he did not even dare to come out with his aggression; only once did he accuse me of trying to force my interpretation upon him. In other words, he projected upon me the role of the aggressive father who had really forced him to accept his opinions without contradiction. In his objection the patient repeated the feeling of being passively overwhelmed (negative, inverted Oedipus complex in feminine identification) and the defense reaction of pseudo aggression. I explained to him that his conscious belief or disbelief was unimportant for us in analysis. However, since he projected the father-repetition upon me, he did not accept that. We see in this case the following prerequisites for the "mechanism of hypocrisy": a very weak and frightened Ego confronted with an authoritarian educator who enforces acceptance of his dictum without contradiction. The first reaction in some cases seems to be a false submissiveness (pseudo submissiveness). That pretense of submission is one of the indispensable features of hypocrisy.[5]

[5]Hypocrisy can be observed as a *transitory* phase in *every* analysis before an interpretation is inwardly accepted. Since in analysis a change in the

After his complaint to my colleague, I was of course interested in determining if hypocrisy was a new acquisition of my patient. Of course it was not; it was only the resuscitation of an old mechanism. His stupidity, widely publicized in his environment, gave him (only unconsciously, to be sure) a queer feeling of superiority: all of these people were convinced that he was stupid, whereas he was cleverly capitalizing on their pity. What happened in analysis in this case was the change from an unconscious to a conscious hypocrisy as a transitory phase. The reason was this: Once more the patient's Ego was confronted with the inescapable superiority of a person who, in his opinion, wanted to force his opinions upon him as his father had once really done. Naïvely the patient assumed that if he did not *consciously* believe my interpretations he simply could not be cured, and he persisted in that misconception despite all my protests. On the other hand, the old situation of pseudo aggression toward his overpowering father was brought to the fore; that was his *modus vivendi*. His first successful attempt to have intercourse was interpreted by him not as a lessening of his neurosis, *but as inner danger*. Since he had lost his symptom, he felt that he was overwhelmed by me via interpretation as once he was overpowered by his father. Therefore he was forced exactly on the day of his success to be aggressive toward me in defense, by complaining to my colleague. Since he wanted to be punished and partly to be passively overwhelmed, he chose this transparent way of achieving his objective with an easily discernible lie.

All of this explains his actions on that for him fateful day, but not his hypocrisy. He was confronted with the fact that he really believed my interpretation; this was his way of explaining his success in coitus. But he could not accept anything in common

---

Super-Ego takes place, it is understandable that the patient uses the old mechanisms of warding off educational authorities. This interpretation fits well with an unpublished remark of Ferenczi to the effect that hypocrisy seems to be a typical transitory phase of childhood. This remark was made to Anna Freud, who quoted it in the discussion of a paper of mine, "The Psychology of Plagiarism," in the Vienna Psychoan. Soc., June 1932. Details are published in that paper, *Psychoanalytische Bewegung*, 1932.

with his father, since that meant, in his unconscious vocabulary, being overwhelmed once more sexually by him. So he chose, once more, the outlet of ironic pseudo acceptance in hypocrisy, giving himself the following advantages: He proved to his unconscious conscience (Super-Ego) that he made fun of his father without depriving himself of the advantage of accepting the interpretation (the loss of his symptom of impotence). Moreover, by this procedure he gave himself the alibi that he was not passively submissive but aggressive toward his father. Stupid or no, here was a neurotic determined to eat his cake and have it too.

The hypocrite, then, is in reality a very passive person desperately trying to prove his "aggression." Small wonder that the neurotic with a money neurosis is predestined to be hypocritical as well, since this is exactly his conflict too.

PART SIX: THE IMPOSTOR AND EMBEZZLER

I swindled people out of money?
So what? The suckers asked for it.

Statement of an impostor

19. IMPOSTOR'S UNCONSCIOUS REASONING: "THEY LOVE MONEY, LET THEM BE PUNISHED BY MONEY."

Neurotic money lovers are so preoccupied with not being taken advantage of that, while watching the pennies, they become easy prey of impostors, embezzlers, confidence men, bankruptcy specialists, check forgers, adventurers who swindle them out of hundreds and thousands of dollars. To complete the irony, the cheat himself does not enjoy his loot for any length of time, but skillfully maneuvers himself into jail. Hence the neurotic cheating of money has no rational aim.

The elastic term "psychopathic personality"

covers the type of person who, as an adult, lives by his wits. This individual has an unconventional approach to money—meaning a complete disregard for the distinctions of mine and thine in money matters. His victims complain bitterly, following their disillusionment, that the cheat made such a good impression. Instead of investigating their own reasons for so willingly opening their pocketbooks to an ingratiating crook, they waste their time and energy in futile complaints.

The actions of the cheating type of money neurotic cannot be explained in terms of rational motives. Gradually, as a result of the dissemination of psychiatric studies, some part of the public is growing more discerning in the matter As an example I quote an article by Albert Deutsch, "12 Mental Quirks in White-Collar Cheats," published on June 3, 1949.

The bizarre case of Banker Richard H. Crowe, who comes up for sentence for having made off with nearly a million dollars of his bank's money, brings to mind some fascinating studies into the minds and personalities of embezzlers and other "white collar" offenders.

The dapper Mr. Crowe, you recall, had first entered a plea of not guilty on grounds of insanity. He was examined by Bellevue Hospital psychiatrists, who pronounced him legally sane. Last week he changed his plea to guilty and threw himself on the mercy of the court.

Crowe is reported to have remarked, shortly after the police apprehended him in Florida:

"I don't know why I did it or what went wrong. Maybe a good psychiatrist or two can figure it out. I can't."

Whether a psychiatrist could help Mr. Crowe is a question now beyond our purview, but the known facts concerning his embezzling act indicate a number of queer motives and methods. To mention just a few: there was the senseless improvisation of the embezzlement, the crude disposal of the funds, the paying of debts through the mails when the culprit knew a police dragnet was out for him, his strange behavior in Florida, the childishly weak effort to cover his tracks and the apparent knowledge from the moment of the theft itself that capture would be inevitable. The case, as noted, recalls some interesting observations by psychiatrists who have made special studies of personality types who commit "white collar crimes." Among these men is Dr. Edmund Bergler, whose informative and entertaining new book, The Basic Neurosis *(Grune and Stratton) includes a discerning chapter on the personality of the "impostor" type.*

Due no doubt to the limitations of space, Mr. Deutsch could give only a brief summary of the results of my investigations: the twelve descriptive characteristics[1] are here presented in full:

1. *Social climbing.* The impostor is "one who imposes upon others by an assumed character or false pretensions" (Webster). Interestingly enough, the term applies only to persons pretending to be more, socially, than they really are; it never includes persons who pretend the opposite. Calif Harun al-Raschid in the disguise of a merchant would not be called an impostor by the admiring crowd if discovered. In German the word *Hochstapler* expresses exactly that social climbing: *hoch* means "high" and the old *stapfen* means "to walk," in other words, "a crook pretending to belong to higher social circles" (Meyer). What the phrase basically refers to is the swindling of money or of social acknowledgment or both through the pretense of being somebody by someone whom—to quote an impostor—the snobbish outerworld would consider a nobody.

2. *Charming, disarming behavior* inspiring confidence by firmness and self-assurance and winning everyone's friendship. Women, especially, are charmed by the occasional feminine trends in these men, finding narcissistically some unconscious similarity to themselves. There are cases on record where a man of this type has married three women, has been sent to jail because of his trigamy and still has not incurred the anger of his wives, because he was so charming.

3. *Sense of humor of specific type.* Among the bag of tricks of the impostor is always a peculiar ironic twist which makes fun of

[1] First presented in "Psychopathology of Impostors," *Journal of Criminal Psychopathology,* V. 2, 1944.

social institutions or prejudices, reducing them to absurdity for his own inner purposes. A classical example is the *cause célèbre* of the "Captain from Koepenick." In 1906 a shoemaker, disguised in the uniform of a Prussian captain, confiscated the municipal money in a suburb of Berlin. He was able to steal this money only because nobody doubted the right of a Prussian officer to do as he pleased; no one was suspicious, since respect for the uniform in the Kaiser's militaristic state was universal. Cleverly capitalizing on that prejudice, the "Captain" even mobilized a whole company of soldiers for his purpose. Ironically enough, the ironic twist in his action brought about his pardon later. On hearing the report of his conduct, the Kaiser laughed and considered it a compliment on his successful education in militaristic respect. The same ironic twist has been psychologically correctly represented in Sascha Guitry's *History of a Cheat.* In it a boy is punished for some puerile cheating by being sent to bed without supper. The next morning the remainder of his family die of poisoned mushrooms eaten the evening before. The irony in this story is that the punishment for good morals is death: the reward for bad morals is survival.

4. *Pseudo-identification mimicry.* The impostor plays the role he has designated for himself with the utmost confidence, as if he really *were* the person he would personify. His identification is that of an actor. On the other hand, he is always aware of his faking, inwardly making fun of the disguise and the people who are taken in by it.

5. *Bombastic braggadocio.* Every impostor presents his faked story convincingly, with or without false modesty; his sureness is the prerequisite for his success. His feigned conviction reminds one superficially of certain childhood lies. However, the fact remains that the impostor never believes his own story; he is full of conscious irony toward the people who believe him, and derives great pleasure from pulling their legs.

6. *Infantile approach toward time.* The impostor does not have the normal person's consideration for the future. His yardstick is today and today's hour only. This tendency is visible, for instance, when he is discovered in his cheating. He maintains ap-

pearances until the last second. In one case a young girl patient was caught, years before entering analysis, attempting to swindle in a store, having given as her name that of a wealthy acquaintance. The store manager faintly remembered the woman whose name she had assumed, and called that woman by phone. Until the last second the girl pretended to be the woman. The manager, and later the judge, were completely at a loss to understand what advantage lay in the continuation of the pretense for a few minutes more, especially since it could serve only as an aggravating circumstance to consider in passing judgment.

7. *Pose of "having a good time" covering depression.* The impostor gives the impression of being an everlasting optimist, and often pretends to himself that he is happy. He derives, to be sure, a good deal of conscious satisfaction from ridiculing his environment, through his successful fake. Below this thin layer of pleasure in irony, deep depression is hidden, sometimes directly visible in the cheat when he is seemingly unobserved.

8. *Inability to enjoy self-created success.* Contrary to popular assumption that the impostor uses cheating for rational purposes, clinical facts prove that he acts irrationally: he neither enjoys his self-created success nor makes use of it for any length of time. One can imagine that a person may use incorrect means for the purpose of achieving success; usually once success is gained in this manner, it is clung to. The impostor, however, overdoes his triumph, seems to get bored with it, and unconsciously provokes his own downfall. He either leaves the place of his temporary success, partly through fear of being exposed, and renews his pattern at another spot, or goes temporarily to jail because of a self-provoked crisis.

9. *"Cynical" and remorseless attitude.* The cynical and pseudoconscienceless philosophy embodied in "So what?" is consciously predominant in the impostor. More, he constantly tries to appear tough, especially when caught. "I married three wives? So what? They were in different places." "I cheated people out of money? So what? Suckers ask for it." "I told fantastic lies about my noble descent? So what? Why were these idiots gullible enough to believe me?" And so on.

10. Stabilization of type of lawbreaking on the cheating level. It is interesting to note that in *typical* cases of cheating no further development in crime is observable; crimes of a more serious character, such as murder, are not committed. The cheat remains a lifelong cheat, repeating his pattern in different disguises over and over.

11. Pathologic approach toward work. The impostor works only in transitory periods, unsually chiefly to gain the confidence of the people he hopes to cheat. He considers work not a necessary means of obtaining a livelihood, but a prerequisite for his schemes of cheating. Consciously he feels superior to slaves who accept work as the natural way of making a living.

12. Incorrigibility. The records of typical impostors show that neither prison nor good advice nor help of any kind changes their behavior. Only psychiatric treatment can, in some cases, change the neurotic disease of the impostor.

These purely descriptive "characteristics" require a genetic explanation. Analysis of a larger group of these psychopaths yielded this result:

Impostors represent a special group of those people who use the "mechanism of criminosis." I shall summarize the essentials of this mechanism: The criminotic represents a specific case of failure to overcome the oral disappointment, one unique in its specific solution. The feeling of pre-oedipal disappointment in the mother and helplessness to take revenge on her for this disappointment force the criminal unconsciously to his herostratic act. His situation is that of a dwarf fighting a giant who refuses to take cognizance of his fight. The only way he can force the giant to recognize his intention is by using dynamite, so to speak, which also destroys him. That tendency to take revenge for oral disappointments in the pre-oedipal mother is projected upon society and is coupled with unconsciously self-intended punishment. *Only unconscious anticipation and acceptance of punishment makes crime possible for the criminal,* since it appeases his inner conscience. The criminal *has* a conscience, and a very severe one. He uses a specific device to appease it—severe self-imposed punishment. In every criminal action two factors are involved, one constant and one variable. The *constant* factor ("mechanism of criminosis") explains the motor act, the real riddle in crime. It is based on the masochistic attempt to overcome the inner feeling of helplessness stemming from pre-oedipal oral conflicts, mentioned above.[2] The *variable* factor pertains to the psychologic contents of the specific crime; it must be determined in every specific case and is as multitudinous as unconscious motivations in general. In my opinion, the social factors in crime play a relatively subordinate role; in the majority of cases they are rationalizations for hidden unconscious motives or the hitching post for masochistic repetition of injustices experienced in reality or fantasy in the child-mother-father relationship, afterward projected and perpetuated masochistically upon society or the social order in general.

Still, the special group of impostors, in itself a subgroup of "narcissistic psychopaths" (sometimes formerly called "moral insanity") has features characteristic of this group alone. Here they are in the order of importance:

1. The narcissism of these sick people is out of proportion, or, more often, cannot overcome its early oral disappointment. To restore that lesion in self-esteem, *the inner, unconscious necessity arises to prove consistently the capacity to inspire love and admiration.* This defense mechanism accounts for the charming and disarming behavior of impostors. But since that proof is only a narcissistic face-saving device, the masochistic *"mechanism of criminosis"* comes to the fore immediately afterward and leads to self-provoked masochistic defeats. The notion often advanced that the narcissistic impostor wants nothing but the admiration that was refused to him in childhood can be disproved easily. Were it true, he would try to achieve such a situation and enjoy

[2] The differential diagnosis between the "mechanism of criminosis" and the "mechanism of orality" cannot be discussed here. The latter consists of the triad: provocation of a refusal; repression of the initial provocation and pseudo aggression, seemingly in self-defense; finally masochistic self-pity. Concerning these mechanisms, the controversial contents or oral regression and the literature, see the author's paper, "Suppositions about the Mechanism of Criminosis," *Journal of Criminal Psychopathology,* 1943.

it. Nothing of the sort happens; after achieving love, he throws it away.

2. Impostors avoid success not only because they want psychic masochistic pleasure but also because they want to offend and *take revenge upon people whom they identify with the mother of the pre-oedipal period*. They want to arouse love and admiration, but having aroused it, they throw it away in order to offend the mother substitute. It is as if they would say: "I only wanted to prove to you that I could get your love—but I don't care to have it."[3]

3. The guilty feeling of impostors stems from masochistic wishes to reduce the mother to absurdity as a giving person and to enjoy unconsciously her refusal. The throwing away of love achieved in later repetitions is in itself a *defense mechanism of pseudo aggression against these deep-seated masochistic wishes* and not simply the result of a feeling of guilt because of that pseudo aggression or oedipal repetition.

4. That unconscious pseudo-aggressive defense mechanism is visible also in the strange sense of humor which impostors use to attack venerable institutions or time-honored prejudices of the environment.

5. The lack of feelings and lack of conscience belong in the same category. *Both are futile attempts to escape psychic masochism*. The wish for punishment finds its expression in a jail term or in the expectation of jail. The impostor's humor represents his frantic attempt to deny that he is narcissistically wounded and therefore depressed.

6. To sum up: the impostor is an oral-parasitic sufferer of criminosis—as are all other criminotics. What distinguishes him from criminotics of other types is an inflated *specific* mechanism to restore his narcissism—the proof that he can be loved. After achieving that proof, he has no use for it and throws it away out of *pseudo aggression*. Since the inner conflict continues, he must prove to himself once more that he can be loved—and so the vicious circle continues ad infinitum. The interruptions of his

[3] A similar tendency may be observed *in dosi refracta* in different narcissistic neurotics.

career by jail are unconsciously self-provoked and self-intended. Whereas the habitual criminal works with intimidation and murderous weapons, the impostor—"the laughing and charming criminal"—works with irony and hurt feelings. Impostors use a *specific device of "self-cure"*: restoration of their narcissism through being loved and admired. That self-cure turns out to be only a self-cure in narcissistic degradation.

Why does the impostor cheat people of money precisely? Why not of women, power, influence or other valuables? The reasons are these:

1. Unconsciously, he continues irony on a childlike level. "You don't love me; you love only money." As a countermove he takes away exactly that possession.

2. Cheating people of money is the surest way to make irreconcilable enemies of them. Even the psychic masochist, who unconsciously wants to be mistreated, uses pseudo aggression and clamors for the sheriff when cheated of money. The impostor takes a sure bet on a jail ticket when he uses money as the tool for his tricks.

3. The moral odium attached to cheating others of money is greater than that of any other offense on a similar level. People forgive almost everything but being cheated of money. Consequently the "negative moral odium" is a part of the masochistically aggravating technique of self-damagement.

Contrary to the reportage of the tabloids, *genital sex* plays a relatively unimportant role in the make-up of the impostor. This fact has been repeatedly observed and described by various authors. Why is this so? First, because the impostor's sex life is immature, full of inner pseudo aggression, pregenital; consequently it never reaches the genital level. Second, because it is subordinated to the one and only driving force of these people—their narcissistic reparation, "I can be loved." Third, because it is subordinated to that narcissistic reparation also in so far as it is scheming, to use a patient's word. It is used as a weapon for neurotic cheating ideas.

Patient A. was interested in the lowest prostitutes only. He cherished unconsciously the idea that perhaps he had syphilis. A few years before entering analysis he was afraid of having contracted syphilis and went to the outpatient department of a hospital for a Wassermann test. He gave his blood under an assumed name, and never inquired about the result. . . . His landlady accused him of stealing in an instance in which he was not guilty. He was arrested, but by chance was able to prove his innocence. He immediately started sexual relations with this old woman.

Patient B. was uninterested in women. He was married, but did not have intercourse with his wife, since she had become distasteful to him because his castration fear was aroused when she had her pubic hair shaved for a gynecological operation. The hair grew back but the patient's castration fear remained and he was practically impotent, though undisturbed by his impotence.

Patient C. played off one girl friend against another continually. He was fully conscious that his relations with women were, as he called it, impersonal. The fact that he was hurting the feelings of his girl friends was a joke to him. To what degree all of his relations were based on unconscious pseudo aggression was proved by the fact that he could ejaculate very quickly with women who needed a longer period of intercourse to be aroused, despite the fact that in general his potency was not weak. During the second intercourse he had aspermia (lack of ejaculation, based on unconscious refusal.) On the superficial level, however, he played an oedipal role, attaching himself to a woman fifteen years his senior, with whom he repeated, under oedipal disguise, the oral conflict, still visible in his aspermia.

Patient D. was a homosexual pervert who used stolen money to buy presents for his friends. He was very ingenious in cheating people of money, pretending to be an investment specialist. Even in his homosexuality he was mainly interested in the enjoyment of being unjustly treated. With every present he wronged his partner, accusing him indirectly, through his gifts, of loving money only. The patient suffered from premature ejaculation in his homosexual relations.

Patient E. was completely frigid, but stated that she felt a queer excitement when engaged in kleptomaniac activities or when pretending to be a rich lady. She was uninterested in genital sexuality, practicing it occasionally only as would a woman spy who wanted to drain the man of some secret, as she put it. It is important to note that in some cases of impostors the oedipal conflict seems to be near the surface. The result has been that even analysts have mistaken that defense for the genetic reason. The real conflict is not oedipal; impostors flee from the "oral danger" (masochistic conflict with the aggressive, "bad" mother of the pre-oedipal time) to the passive and harmless mother of the oedipal period. Proof of this fact that impostors are orally fixated or regressed to the oral phase can be found in some of their symptoms: lack of interest in genital sexuality, with preference for perversions, for instance homosexuality; in their neurotic symptoms, for example ejaculation praecox, aspermia, etc. —all orally conditioned disturbances.

The impostor is a typical victim of the "mechanism of criminosis" with one specific distinguishing characteristic: the attempt to restore in his defense mechanism a lesion of his narcissism. Everything also is subordinated to the goal of providing a defense for himself—that he can make people love him. The real, dynamically effective masochistic wish is repressed. The moment he has achieved the proof, the love itself becomes unimportant and the chase for narcissistic reparation, interrupted by jail sentences, begins anew. This narcissistic technique of the impostor reminds me—*mutatis mutandis*—of a patient who was narcissistically hurt over the fact that he was incapable of producing an erection. After a few months of analysis, he proudly announced to me that the night before he had had an erection while he was in bed with his virginal wife. "What did you do with that erection?" I asked. "What do you mean?" he inquired in surprise. "Well, did you attempt intercourse or were you satisfied with the erection in itself?" "The latter," was the patient's laconic reply.

Very interesting is the conclusion reached by impostors that good morals are generally lacking in business. It is obvious that, for purposes of self-defense, they must draw a dark picture. A few of these patients stated their views as follows: "Crookedness in business seldom makes the headlines, though it is the order of the day. Most of the good people have no scruples about fina-gling, lying, and double-crossing. The only remarkable thing is their moral indignation if the other fellow proves to be smarter than they." One such man declared: "To be smart in business seldom means having a new idea which makes money because it is new. To be smart means in general to be a better bluffer, cheat, and double-crosser than the other fellow. I don't mind these honorable people being cutthroats—that's natural in business competition. What I mind is their pious hypocrisy." Another summarized his impressions as follows: "It is amazing with what ease the good citizen will perjure himself by taking *any* oath, to save a few hundred dollars. He will lie his head off in court, swear he never saw you; he never got your merchandise; you never gave him the information which you actually did give him; in short, call black white and white black. After his perjury he will come to you, shake your hand, and be surprised if you turn your back. Then he will say indignantly that you're not a good sport. All these lies go under the heading of business."

Now it cannot be denied that the description is accurate—but with one reservation: it applies only to individuals of their *own* type, since in every field of endeavor psychopaths are represented in a higher percentage than is generally assumed. By focusing their attention on psychopathic behavior and implying that it is universal, impostors draw the conclusion that crookedness and business are synonymous, and thus they diminish their guilt feel-ings. When one listens to their tirades, one gets the impression that they really believe they are the best people to conduct a crusade against crooked business morals. "*Gracchi de seditione querentes.*"

Wittels sums up very precisely the prevailing psychoanalytic opinions concerning the therapy of impostors: "We are not as yet very efficient in the treatment and cure of criminal psychopaths. Regular psychoanalysis can be of some help, but rarely, because the transference necessary in this work is unreliable and desul-tory with these patients."

In addition to the difficulty of achieving a workable transference, other factors complicate the problem of impostors. First, these men never enter analysis of their own volition. Second, if they come at all they do so under pressure of their desperate families, who pay and pay (for instance, for forged checks, debts illegitimately contracted, etc.) to keep the criminotic out of trouble and who try analysis as a last resort. Third, every analysis "made to order" (Freud) has a bad prognosis to start with. It is, of course, theoretically possible to mobilize the latent and misplaced unconscious feeling of guilt for therapeutic purposes; practically, however, the chances are very slim indeed. With stoicism, cynicism, or hypocrisy the criminotic accepts all of the statements concerning threatening jail sentences, social disgrace, family grief, etc., without changing his course. Fourth, it happens sometimes, though rarely, that a patient of this type enters treatment because of some other neurotic symptom, for instance, impotence, neurotic headache, hypochondriacal symptoms, etc. Indirectly we are thus given the possibility of analyzing his whole personality. However, he brings forth the greatest objections to "dragging in things that are nobody's business," to quote such a patient. Fifth, the cases we see are never clear-cut; in general they are mixed cases. A combination of impostor features with gambling, alcoholism, drug addiction, kleptomania, homosexuality are common. The patient singles out one pet symptom and refuses to analyze anything else. Sixth, the general instability of psychopaths results, even among those who enter analysis voluntarily, in their treating the whole procedure as a joke and often running away the moment they come to understand, even for a short time, the seriousness of their situation. "I understood yesterday, for the first time, what you really are after," said a kleptomaniac patient. "You want to make a good citizen of me. There is no fun in that for me. Good-by!"

After having had repeatedly the same experience as many of my colleagues, that it is nearly impossible to mobilize the guilt feelings of impostors through the channels of transference, I no longer try to mobilize these feelings in the *beginning* of analysis. I now start immediately to point out the ridiculousness of their constant attempt to restore their narcissism as it manifests itself in their specific defense mechanism, "I can achieve love," covering their deep masochistic attachment. The result is that it is possible to keep such patients in analysis at least for some time. Furious and ironic objections at once begin; these patients are vulnerable at one point—fear of appearing ridiculous. *There* their narcissism comes into play, and whereas previously *all* of my analyses of impostors ended more or less without any success, in general being terminated by the patient's refusal to continue treatment, now my experience is more favorable. In a series of cases patients have been helped, a few even to a degree which one could, euphemistically, call something like a cure. There is, however, in general no reason at all to be overoptimistic about the results of treatment of impostors; quite the contrary. Still, I believe that the mechanism described above gives us not only some clues to the understanding of the impostor's unconscious but also the beginning of a therapy of his queer disease.

Where logic ends, the unconscious takes over.

From the author's *Unhappy Marriage and Divorce*[1]

20. SENSELESS STEALING: KLEPTOMANIA

People who like to explain all peculiarities in money matters on rational grounds—"a dollar is a dollar" —are quite at a loss when confronted by kleptomania. Typical, normal stealing they profess to understand: the aim, though dangerous, seems rational. In kleptomania the aim doesn't make sense: a lady of means who could charge anything she likes in a department store but who instead shoplifts a dress seems to the rationalists to be slightly insane.

[1]Int. Universities Press, 1946.

The logical approach to both typical and atypical stealing starts off on the wrong foot. The yardstick in both cases is the advantage to be gained from the act of stealing. What confuses the rationalists is the faulty assumption that a seemingly rational act must have a rational reason behind it. The fact is that pseudo rationality may be used as a blind to cover unconscious and fully irrational reasons.

To begin with, stealing in an organized society is an irrational act, whatever its seeming motivation. Popular anger against the thief, combined with excellently organized law enforcement agencies, makes it pretty certain that the theif will not get away with it. Hence an offense perpetrated against overwhelming odds smacks of pseudo rationality, the real motivation being the unconscious wish to be caught.

The problem of criminosis,[2] the special subdivision of neurotic-psychopathic actions to which stealing belongs, is extremely complex and not fully settled. Scientific differences of opinion are rampant. All psychiatric investigations agree that an unconscious substructure does exist. That the substructure is not so simple as the layman assumes is shown in an interesting incident which occurred a few years ago when two psychiatrists devoted several months to an investigation, conducted in prison, of cases of stealing. The experiment was made public, and had, among others, this result: a young man, hearing of the possibility of being psychoanalyzed in prison, *gave himself up in order to be analyzed.* There were warrants out for his arrest, and he received a two-year prison sentence and actually entered psychoanalysis but discontinued it, with a number of threadbare excuses, after a short time.[3]

It is impossible, within the framework of this book, to discuss criminosis. My personal opinions are included in *The Battle of the Conscience,* in a longer chapter entitled "The Neurotic Who

[2]The term was first suggested by Dr. A. N. Foxe, to whom psychiatric criminology is indebted for a series of important contributions, and has since become a part of psychiatric nomenclature.

[3]Alexander and Healy, *Roots of Crime,* Knopf, 1935.

Unconsciously Bargains for the Electric Chair: The Criminal."[4] However, it may be stated in passing that in every criminal action *two* factors have to be distinguished: the *psychologic content* and the *motor act*. A large part of scientific literature is based on conclusions overlooking that fact; thus the psychologic contents present in neurosis do not explain why, in criminosis, an *overt* act is resorted to rather than unconscious defenses being produced in neurotic symptoms only. The issue is further confused by dissension over the question of whether unconscious wishes or (as I believe) only defenses come to the fore. Finally, it suffices to state my contention that a specific unconscious technique is used by the criminotic to appease his *severe* conscience; the criminotic act is unconsciously permitted because punishment is "calculated in." Hence it is that so many criminotics betray themselves by their own mistakes, and that the ratio of detected to undetected crimes is so overwhelmingly in favor of the former.

Kleptomania is one of the more harmless criminoses, but the family burdened with a member who is a kleptomaniac is tragically involved, because social status is at stake. One might say that kleptomania is a disease of the wealthy. Frequently the family forces the kleptomaniac into psychiatric treatment.

The motivations of the psychologic aspect of kleptomania are by no means to *get* the specific stolen object, which frequently

[4]The chapter gives the contents of a long series of investigations: "Suppositions about the Mechanism of Criminosis," *Journal of Criminal Psychopathology*, V. 2, 1943; "Psychopathology of Impostors," ibid., V. 4, 1944; "Eight Prerequisites for Psychoanalytic Treatment of Homosexuality," *Psychoanalytic Review*, 31:3, 1944; "The Respective Importance of Reality and Phantasy in the Genesis of Female Homosexuality," *Journal of Criminal Psychopathology*, V. 1, 1943; "Hypocrisy—Its Implications in Neurosis and Criminal Psychopathology," ibid., IV, 1943; "The Psychology of Gambling," *Imago*, 1936; "The Gambler—A Misunderstood Neurotic," *Journal of Criminal Psychopathology*, IV, 3, 1943; "Problems of Suicide," *The Psychiatric Quarterly Supplement*, 20:2, 1946; and "Applications of the Mechanism of Orality in Neurosis and Criminosis," *Handbook of Correctional Psychology*, edited by Lindner and Seliger, Philosophical Library, New York, 1947; "Crime and Punishment," *The Psychiatric Quarterly Supplement*, 21:2, 1947.

has an unconscious meaning. On the contrary, the wish to get is but an inner defense against the masochistic wish to be refused. The getting desire is acted upon as an unconscious defense.

I experienced the deepest low in my life while rid-
ing on a train to Philadelphia; I was to report the
next day for my new position in the South, and I
had to face the fact that on the same day some of
my forged checks would be discovered by the
people in New York whose signatures I had forged.
I was in despair—I didn't know where to turn. Yet
at that moment I noticed that, in some peculiar
way, I was not unhappy at all. . . .

Statement of a patient

21. COMBINATION TYPE OF MONEY NEUROSIS

Every textbook simplifies the complexity of material by subdividing it neatly into chapters. The
living patient is frequently less obliging; without
even asking permission, he combines different chapters in one.

For instance, a gambler is forced by his family to
enter treatment because, in order to pay his debts,
he has forged checks. At the same time this man
suffers from ulcers of the stomach, a psychosomatic
disease.

Another man, suffering from kleptomania, is

forced by a relative to consult the psychiatrist. He does not consider himself sick at all. In a few days, however, the picture becomes complicated by a few new admissions: the patient is
burdened by (a) pathologic gambling, (b) check forging, (c)
potency disturbance, (d) perversion "coprophemia," denoted
by, in this specific variation, the whispering of obscene words
when passing women on the street.

A third man enters analysis because of homosexuality. He then
states: "To combat my depression following homosexual acts, I
started to drink. To combat that vice, I began to gamble. To
combat both, I decided to marry—and found myself impotent. . . ."

And so on, in ever new variations, combinations, and permuta-
tions.

The confusing array becomes clarified the moment one understands that all these diversified clinical pictures represent but
frantic attempts at expressing, and at the same time combating,
the basic trouble: psychic masochism. The end result is always
the same—jail, or, at the very least, danger of social disgrace. Of
course the individual *specific* reasons for picking exactly the
specific difficulties have very personalized reasons in the unconscious make-up of *individual defenses*.

A good-looking woman in the early thirties was chaperoned
into my office by a very considerate husband. The lady immediately retired behind her handkerchief; the husband told the
sorry tale. According to him, his wife, always a happy and normal person, had, during the last year, become moody and depressed. She suffered from crying spells; physicians called her
symptoms—for which she herself could offer no explanation—a
case of nerves. Tactfully, after finishing his little speech, the husband left my office, having assured me that the marriage was
perfect, and requested immediate treatment of his wife, which,
he added, he was quite capable of financing.

As soon as he had gone, the lady's tearful facial expression of
despondency vanished and she asked in a businesslike way:

"Now can we talk turkey?"

I assured her that we could.

"With medical secrecy guaranteed?"

"You know the law."

"How can I be sure you won't use me, some day, as 'illustrative material' in a book or a case history?"

"If that should happen, you will be disguised so as to be unrecognizable."

"What will you make out of me? A lascivious Française?"

"Do you consider that your problem?"

This time the tears were less theatrical. When she had stopped crying she told part of her story. After a few years of dull marriage to a harmless bore she had decided that life must have something more than this in store for her, and had begun a few affairs just to find out whether frigidity was a woman's lot or the fault of the husband. Her exploits were meagerly rewarding, although she experienced more than in the marital bed. Analyzing her feelings, she decided that the plus factor in extramarital affairs was connected, not with specific men, but with the mystery of danger. From this she concluded that a good mystery story, written intelligently so that the reader could identify with the central character, would be less dangerous and equally rewarding. But the substitution did not work. Disappointed, she blamed poor writing for the failure; then, deciding that the trouble was due to lack of real action in stories, she stopped being angry with the mystery writers. Meanwhile, her husband, the harmless bore, had become quite successful and she more interested in keeping him. He, however, had heard rumors about her affairs, and now he became suspicious, made a terrific row and threatened divorce. She attempted to convince him that the rumors were tricks engineered by his business competitors and executed via their wives; he swallowed that story only partially, so to allay his suspicions she began to act the sickly, nervous person, and throughout the following year had managed to fool even a few specialists.

At this point in her story the lady interrupted herself and asked ironically: "What is my problem, Doctor?"

"I am not a crystal gazer."

"Well, guess anyhow."

"Obviously it is not your marital situation, which you handle along conventionally tricky—though slightly outmoded—lines."

"Then what *is* my problem?"

"My guess is that it has something to do with your newly discovered mystery of danger. I would suspect, first, gambling, and later involvement with people who——"

I paused, and the patient said in a strained voice: "Well, why don't you finish your sentence?"

"Do you insist?"

"Yes, go ahead."

"Involvement with the criminal element in gambling—to pay your gambling debts."

A long silence followed. At last the woman said tonelessly: "How come?"

"Wait a minute. This whole discussion, as arranged by you, is irregular. *You* are supposed to give information, remember?"

"I just want to see how much can be deduced from the information I have given you."

"You wish to make a psychological intelligence test, is that it? My deduction is simple to the point of banality: you said you became interested in the mystery of danger and then found that imaginary danger, via identification, would not do. The next step was deciding that action was the missing ingredient. It is impossible that you could become immediately involved in gangsterism. I also excluded—for the moment—the possibility that you had taken up any dangerous addictions. Therefore, by a process of elimination, I reached the conclusion that the thrill of gambling might be next on your list. But if you had been successful you would never have consented to consulting a psychiatrist, for how could you be sure he wouldn't tell your husband you were faking? Agreeing to consult me, as your husband requested, meant you had some *good* reason for being treated—and for wanting medical secrecy."

"Yes, but what interests me is why you made that allusion to my being mixed up with gangster-gamblers?"

"Protracted gambling leads to losing."

"Invariably?"

"Invariably. And having lost, you needed more money. You told me your husband had started to rebel, so you couldn't have approached him. Result: you are in the hands of gambling gangsters who have you under their thumb. A simple and banal deduction, not worth the fee your husband will have to pay."

"But why didn't you assume that the crook simply forced me to become his mistress?"

"That deduction *is* worth the money your husband will pay. That deduction, you see, is possible only on the basis of specialized knowledge. In your ironic questions concerning secrecy, you asked me whether I would make out of you a lascivious Française. Now, unconscious wishes never come to the fore directly, only in the form of defenses. The unconscious personality works after the principle of admission of the lesser crime. When you were ready to admit to lasciviousness, it automatically meant that was not your real crime."

"I see I'll have to come clean, to use gangster slang. Your suspicion is correct—except that my situation is even worse than you described. The man who holds my notes—and they come to around forty thousand dollars—uses me as a hostess in his exclusive gambling place. I tried to break away, but by employing threats, he forced me to forge my husband's signature to the checks. More precisely, *he* did it in my presence, warning me that he could then say quite truthfully that *I* had committed the forgery. I live in constant fear that some of his gambling customers will recognize me. And, to add to my humiliation, he acts in the presence of these people as if I were his girl friend."

"Did you also try that way out?"

"I did. He proved to be impotent."

"Have you consulted a lawyer?"

"Yes—a good one. His advice was to tell my husband. He refused—for my protection—to take any action behind my husband's back, claiming that my husband's ignorance of the situation would deprive a lawyer of his strongest argument."

"Did he advise anything else?"

"He said I should immediately sever relations with this gambler."

"Will you promise not to be offended if I offer another suspicion?"

"I'm not the touchy type."

"I suspect that you can't untangle yourself—because you *love the danger of your situation.*"

The lady did not answer.

"And I suspect that your own half understanding of that fact is what made you agree to consult me."

She still remained silent.

"In other words, you are powerless to break away from a masochistic allure—that is your problem."

"Can this be changed?"

"Perhaps."

"But you are not sure?"

"Psychic masochism is the greatest, most dangerous poison known to mankind. If you are asking whether, in general, analysis can cure that psychic cancer, the answer is a precise yes. If, however, you mean specifically: 'Can *my specific* masochism be cured?' the answer is a question mark. It depends on the unconscious reactions you will show in treatment. In any case, it is worth a trial."

"I'll try."

"Fine."

"Have you anything to add?"

"Only one thing. Has it occurred to you that your whole trouble started with frigidity? You did not mention that or request a change—but if you were not frigid you would have saved yourself all those progressive steps in your school of danger."

"Do you consider me to be basically a case of frigidity?"

"Not at all. Your frigidity is part and parcel of your craving for failure, hence psychic masochism. What you tried to do was the equivalent of substituting a gangster film, let us say, for a symphony concert: you can see that that would never work. I mention your frigidity merely to point out how much room for improvement there is for you."

"My load of troubles is heavy enough for me as it is."

After arranging for appointment hours, the lady inquired with grim humor: "By the way, if you are so clever, can you describe my torturer?"

"Do you mean his physical characteristics? No, I cannot. But I can tell you something about his personality. He is an *inner weakling* who acts tough and brutal because he has found someone even weaker. Hence your lawyer is right: this man will be intimidated if confronted with a person stronger than himself. All psychic masochists are as putty in the hands of stronger people, and brutal with those who are weaker. Finally—you are overdoing the argument of cleverness. There is no cleverness involved here; unconscious troubles cannot be solved by cleverness and figuring all the angles. All that is required is specialized knowledge."

Upon leaving, the lady said laughingly: "I fooled you, anyway. I wasn't trying to make a psychological intelligence test, as you assumed; I just wanted to find out whether you would be morally indignant. That's what worried me. However, you passed your test."

"I'm sorry to disappoint you, but every patient does that. I once treated a kleptomaniac who argued his head off to prove that I considered him a crook and was morally indignant about it. All my protests that I considered him just a sick person were of no avail. One day he made *his* test: he brought me a present—a valuable book—and informed me from where he had stolen it. The purpose of this procedure was twofold: to catch me off guard by emotionally protesting that he wished to make me his accomplice, and then to force me into indignantly refusing acceptance of the gift. I thanked him politely for the present and suggested analyzing the reasons for his magnanimity. It was possible to convince him that *that* book, at least, should be returned to its owner."

"So you are wise to my tricks? Well, we shall see."

"I accept the challenge."

PART SEVEN: THE DEPENDEE

Weep on! and, as thy sorrows flow,
I'll taste the luxury of woe.

THOMAS MOORE

22. DEPENDEE'S CREED: "DON'T ASK WHY —THE WORLD OWES ME A LIVING."

The dependee[1] is a neurotic who with great regularity maneuvers himself into a position of dependence upon another person, or group of persons, only to complain of the bitter disappointment the ungrateful, inconsiderate attitude of the tight-pursed provider has caused him. It is of no consequence to him that the provider never asked to be appointed to that position, and in fact objects to the burden: the provider not only dispenses money but is also a provider of injustices, and as such is invaluable to the dependee.

[1]The word was coined by Benjamin Stolberg.

The rationalizations of the dependee vary. He may be a dependee on ideological or artistic grounds—isn't he a fighter for a cause, or an artist, with a clear right to ask for support? He may be simply the poor relation of a rich man, in which case it is surely unjust that he should starve while the rich relative lives in luxury. Or he may be in the class of the *Schnorrer,* the perpetual beggar who believes that he does others a favor in letting them support him, thus straightening out their accounts with God.

It is incorrect to call all dependees parasites. Some are, at least sporadically, hard workers. But the earnings from their chosen work do not fill the stomach regularly; therefore in lean periods friends and acquaintances are called on for help. If they fail to respond, or respond to too small a degree to suit the would-be dependee, the great lament starts. Rather grotesquely, the dependee has—ostensibly—a high degree of naïveté concerning the benevolence of human nature. This pseudo naïveté is part and parcel of the (unconsciously) sought-for disappointment.

At the other end of the scale is the dependee without ideological or artistic rationalizations. Here the term parasite is hard to avoid, though the surface description is inadequate, for the parasite has a psychology of his own. The role of dependee, as distinguished from that of *dependent,* is, in our society, mainly a masculine prerogative; it is the accepted custom for the female of the species to be taken care of in legal marriage.

Despite flimsy and sometimes slightly paranoiac rationalizations, the basic structure of all dependees is the unconscious masochistic wish to be refused. The rationalizations are hard to break through, but when cornered the dependee will admit that he feels the world owes him a living. "Don't ask me why," shouted such a patient indignantly. "I have a right to live my life!" "At others' expense," I remarked dryly. The patient retorted with a single word: "Bourgeois!"

In analyzing people of this type, one finds in superficial layers this peculiar parasitism. Typically, the wish to *get* corresponds *seemingly* to repetition of the infantile situation where the child's needs were taken care of. This, however, is a mirage. Without masochistic elaboration, the dependee would have "learned his lesson"—that in this "cruel world" one has to earn his living. The stubborn clinging to the infantile idea of having to be supported is obviously more acceptable to the dependee than the deeper repressed masochistic substructure.

23. EVERY ABSURDITY HAS A CHAMPION TO DEFEND IT[1]

Reduced to the simplest common denominator, all dependees are masochistic seekers of disappointment, with variable parts of their Ego intact. These parts determine to what degree work can be accomplished, at least sporadically. Characteristically, even if the dependee works, he refuses stubbornly to make any concessions to the prevailing market. He insists that he can produce only in his specific field of interest; and if the product is neither wanted nor salable, "it is just too bad for the stupid world."

[1]Oliver Goldsmith.

The propelling reason for this irrational insistence is a duality of factors; the specific work corresponds to an unconscious defense mechanism and thus squares the dependee with his inner conscience by providing refutations and alibis; this sector temporarily appeased, the dependee lives out—with the defensive cover of pseudo aggression—his magnificent psychic masochism. The defensive pseudo aggression makes him bitter, accusing, demanding. According to this peculiar psychic formula, the outer world is obliged to support the dependee. The result is a complete lack of logical thinking as to the reasons why the other fellow should support the dependee. The dependee goes around with an inwardly good conscience: for doesn't he suffer enough? "I've done my share, now do yours," is his unexpressed idea.

THE IDEOLOGICAL DEPENDEE

> *Faith is to believe what we do not see; and the reward of this faith is to see what we believe.*
>
> ST. AUGUSTINE

Ideology covers a wide field, from sectarianism to politics, from propaganda to crackpot-ism. All propagandists of a new idea, provided they are capable of collecting enough adherents, present their claims to support from their followers in the holy name of the cause. The cause may change; the claims remain. Since every absurdity finds its champion, the ideologic dependee, as an institution, is always with us.

Instead of adducing the familiar example of the political dependee, I shall present the faddists—all the more convincing as examples, for the very reason that their cults have no appreciable public backing.

One patient of this type was executive secretary of a nudist club which spread its propaganda in a highly conservative community. The man came for treatment because of potency disturbance. Very soon he started to convince me of the advantages of nudism. I asked him:

"Why do you waste your time in proselytizing? Don't forget, you're doing it on your own time, hence at your own expense. Isn't that in contradiction to your usual procedure?"

"Am I too sensitive, or do I detect a note of irony?"

"Your hearing is perfect."

"What's wrong with my profession?"

"Profession is an elastic word. Didn't you tell me that you failed at several different kinds of business, from a candy store to an auto repair shop?"

"I found my real vocation late in the game."

"Your vocation seems to be that of talking and letting other people support you."

"I resent that. You have no idea of the amount of work involved in my job. I have speeches to deliver, meetings to organize, letters to write, and what not. I have to fight with unbelievers. As a matter of fact, it's a twenty-four-hour-a-day job."

"Do you believe the nonsense you sell?"

"It isn't nonsense. I am selling health. Why, don't you know——"

"Are you starting your propaganda speech again? Better tell me what right you have to be supported by the neurotic suckers you organize."

"I work for the cause, don't I? How can I spend every hour of the day doing this work and still worry about making a living?"

"Do you really believe in your rationalization?"

"Meaning what—nudism or salary?"

"Both."

"Nudism is my belief. I suppose *you* call that fanaticism."

"And your salary?"

"The cause comes first. What's wrong with getting checks from people who are willing to help the cause? The cause has to be organized."

"But do you organize nudists—or your salary checks?"

"You've just got the wrong focus. At bottom I'm a firm believer in the cause. That being the case, I have to live. To live I have to be taken care of."

"Why not reverse the sentence? 'To be taken care of I have to work for the cause.' "

"I resent that."

"Better analyze the reason for your dependeeism."

"How can I be a parasite when I work so hard?"

"What is productive about your work? Is it productive to give neurotics the opportunity of doing the officially forbidden?"

"I am not responsible for the silly taboos of our society."

"You are just exploiting those taboos. And before you repeat your favorite phrase: 'I resent that,' I say again—better analyze your parasitism."

"What has all this talk to do with my potency troubles?"

"A good deal. Your parasitism and your sex troubles are interconnected. In sex it is necessary to *give,* and how can you give if —as seems apparent—you constantly want only to *be given?*"

"Are you implying that I want to be paid for sex too? I can prove you're wrong. I once had an affair with a woman who showered me with gifts—and I was still impotent."

"You misunderstand. Your trouble is not parasitism per se. The parasitism, in fact, is an inner fake defense. What you really want—of course, unconsciously—is to be refused. That is counteracted by the defense: I want to get. If you get, you still feel cheated—in your own estimation, you get too little. Am I wrong in assuming that you consider your salary as organizer of this nudist group too meager?"

"No, you're right. These stingy people just about provide the necessities of life, and that's all."

"There you are—you feel unjustly treated!"

"That's a fact."

"If it's a fact, why don't you change that fact?"

"I'm fighting for an increase in salary."

"I didn't mean that. Why don't you, for a change, do some productive work in a reasonable field of endeavor?"

"There you go again! My present work *is* productive. It gives a lot of people satisfaction—and of course infuriates a lot more."

"Translate: 'I live off organized pseudo aggression.' That's exactly where your sex trouble comes in: you refuse sexual pleasure to a woman; that in turn makes you impotent. Of course the whole problem is insoluble without going into your infantile history, attachments, defenses. Your nudism fad is no less infantile in origin; we will come to that. What interests me at the moment is this: where do you get your silly conviction that you have a right to be supported?"

"I work for these people, so they have to compensate me for my time."

"Why don't you make a phonograph record of that theme of yours? There's no use repeating over and over what you've already told me for weeks. What we want is to ferret out the unconscious reasons."

"You seem to think that *your* job consists of depriving me of mine."

"My job is to restore your potency. That can't be achieved without analyzing your whole personality."

"My personality is O.K. My potency problem is the only difficulty I have."

"That is naïve. Your personality and your potency problem are interconnected. By the way, has it occurred to you that you are the victim of one of your own slogans? You told me repeatedly that it's only in the dirty minds of dirty people that nudism is a sexy problem, whereas *you* proclaim the beauty of the naked body completely free of any sexual connotations. Hasn't your conscience played a diabolical joke on you by saying: 'No sex? Fine —no sex!' "

"I was impotent before I became a nudist."

"That proves my point, because it was one of the factors that propelled you into that faddism."

"Do you go so far as to claim that all our male members are impotent?"

"Something wrong with their sex life, yes. That doesn't necessarily mean impotence alone.[2] Let's go back to your right to be supported."

"I told you the reasons."

"You repeated a few rationalizations which are so shaky that

[2] See *Neurotic Counterfeit Sex,* Grune & Stratton, 1951.

you are forced, in order to silence your own inner disbelief, to proclaim them as sacred convictions."

"I hold my ground."

"Very shaky ground."[3]

Another patient, analyzed a good many years ago, was a psychologist who, disgusted with officialdom, became an adherent of a new pseudo-psychological school, considered by serious psychologists and serious medical men to be on the lunatic fringe. Amusingly enough, when confronted with his own potency troubles, he consulted a scientific enemy.

"Isn't that rather inconsistent?" I wanted to know.

"I can't admit to my troubles in our circles. I have my reputation to consider; I am one of the most important people in the movement."

"I see. Are you a paid official?"

"In a minor way, yes."

"Why did you give up your previous work as a test psychologist?"

"I hated it and worked only sporadically."

"Who supported you?"

"Well, nobody. My wife inherited some money——"

"And what happened to the money?"

"She still has it."

"But I take it she refuses to support you."

"Not exactly. Well, we had conflicts."

"About your supporting yourself?"

"That's practically what it amounted to."

"Do I understand that as an *adult* you were for a time supported by your wife? For how long, by the way?"

"A good many years. You make it sound so degrading—I always considered her money *our* money."

---

[3] The patient ran away from analysis after a few weeks. A month later he came back, introducing himself this time as a salesman for men's underwear. Asked why he now dressed the bare body, where heretofore he had been so stout in the defense of nudism, he said that a specific experience (being beaten while nude by an enemy of the movement) had changed his "outlook on life."

"Very convenient. To clarify the issue: first you were supported by your wife——"

The patient interrupted: "You don't understand. I was studying at that time."

"For a good many years? Wasn't your studying just an alibi? Well, first you were supported by your wife; when she rebelled you took your job, which you hated and at which, therefore, you could work, as you say, only sporadically. Finally you gave that up too, and again became a dependee—this time of your new movement."

"It sounds like an indictment the way you put it. It wasn't so bad really."

"But the facts are indisputable?"

The man did not answer. He came very much to life, however, when asked whether he really believed in the aims of the movement. It turned out that he was a real fanatic, constantly stressing the great work of the founder of that fringe movement. His fanatical admiration for this man gave the impression that he was unconsciously homosexually attached to him. His psychological naïveté was remarkable. He also attacked me quite bitterly for opposing the movement.

This patient was the personification of circumlocution. He could not be made to focus on his problem but talked in circles around it. Precise questions were answered after the principle of: Q. "What time is it?" A. "Friday." Finally I asked him:

"What is your rationalization for having been an eternal supportee?"

"I'm a hard worker."

"I asked about your parasitism. Please answer the question."

"I can prove that I work hard. Besides, our cause——"

"Stop evading the issue. Why are you a chronic dependee?"

"I see we speak a different language."

"Again you avoid the issue. Why do you have to be supported?"

"Because I fight for our movement."

"You were supported by your wife before your so-called movement was ever known to you."

"What's wrong with letting other people work?"

"Essentially you are a sick man. Your cynicism in money matters is no less neurotic than your potency disturbance. The impotence and the money neurosis are interconnected."

"Don't say that I'm cynical. I am a serious person!"

"What is serious about being a lifelong parasite? What's serious about associating yourself with a movement considered by the best medical and psychological authorities to be a sheer unadulterated fake? And tell me what is serious about throwing away an academic degree, your Ph.D., to compromise yourself in the eyes of your own profession? Why is there always something, let's say dubious, about your actions?—using the bourgeois yardstick as a basis for judgment. Especially as your luxurious way of life—made possible by your wife—makes it apparent that you *accept* that yardstick."

"Many new ideas were first rejected by contemporary science. Take your own science, psychoanalysis."

"The fact that there is an unavoidable incubation period for every new idea does not prove that every new idea is rejected *only* because it is new. If someone conceives the idea that the moon is made of green cheese, rejection of the idea will not be solely on the basis of its newness."

"Who is to judge?"

"Posterity—and the subjective conviction of the idea's adherents, provided they are capable of judgment on an intellectual and *not* an affective basis. Apply this to your case. Does it augur well for your so-called convictions that, confronted with a neurotic difficulty, you ask for help from a representative of a science you and your colleagues attack so maliciously? Do you call that *serious* conviction?"

"I have no need of your opinion. Please stick to my real trouble!"

"Your real trouble is your neurotic personality as demonstrated by your money neurosis."

"Don't forget my impotence."

"I suspect that you are so much interested in your potency disturbance chiefly because your wife insists on sex and you are

afraid that unless the problem is solved she will throw you over-
board; obviously she is not prepared to condone parasitism *and*
impotence. Didn't you tell me she has already rebelled against the
first difficulty?"

Of course the patient did not admit that; however, his analysis
proved that the suspicion was justified.

THE ARTISTIC DEPENDEE

> *Of Dr. Goldsmith he said, No man was more foolish*
> *when he had no pen in his hand, or more wise when*
> *he had.*
>
> BOSWELL's *Life of Doctor Johnson*, Vol. II, p. 336

All writers—and the paradigm is applicable to every type of
artistic creativity—are unconsciously chronic defendants accused
before the high tribunal of the inner conscience. In his work, the
productive writer produces a disclaimer, an unconscious alibi, to
be presented to the ogre of his conscience. If he is a writer of
talent, his work corresponds to Robert Gilfillan's theory: Poetry
is truth dwelling in beauty. Truth here refers to the creative
writer's ability to present unconscious facts psychologically correctly, whether he fictionalizes, dramatizes, lyricizes, or satirizes
his material. Beauty, in this formula, hints at secondary elaboration, adorning and expressing the crude unconscious defensive
material in a form enjoyable to the reader. The specific conditions
enabling specific people to employ this particular self-cure of their
neurotic inner conflicts has been dealt with at length in my book,
The Writer and Psychoanalysis.

Writing is thus an unconscious business deal between the accusing inner conscience and the inner lawyer of the unconscious personality—the unconscious Ego. The outer world, it goes without
saying, is totally unconcerned with the writer's inner conflicts: in
a competitive society, only cash counts; and unfortunately the
writer's work, except in rare instances, cannot support its producer. Hence writers with some parts of their Ego intact are

aware that the daily bread must be earned by means of some tangential profession. These are comparatively few, however; the majority of writers cannot adapt themselves to that painful and regrettable fact, and so they become dependees. Their theme song is a bitterly bewildered: "It can't be true because it shouldn't be true"—but mourning over unsalability and inadequate monetary rewards does not change the simple fact that artistic endeavor in most cases does not support the artist.

The history of literature and observation of contemporary poets show with tragic monotony the helpless fight against the brutal truth: creative writing is an inner necessity for the writer, not a way of earning one's living. The artist who does not accept this statistically proven fact becomes of necessity a dependee.

The case of Heinrich Heine, whose genius was beyond question, is a classical example:

The villain of the piece is the uncle who was so constantly and soundly provoked by Heine, and the setting of the conflict is in the tradition of classical comedy: the uncle was a millionaire banker, the poet-nephew a classic parasite, judged by his uncle's standards. Heine demanded a pension from his uncle: he had no real argument in favor of such a pension being given him, except the injustice of the fact that wealth is unequally distributed.

What follows is not, obviously, presented for purposes of evaluation; Heine is acknowledged by everyone, myself included, to be one of the greatest lyricists in world literature. We are here concerned solely with the pathological phenomenon of the poet's dependeeism.

On the occasion of Heine's first visit to London his uncle gave him a letter of credit (about four hundred pounds) with the miserly stipulation that the money was not to be spent: it was to be used merely for the enchancement of the young man's reputation. Heine promptly cashed in the letter of credit and spent the money. The uncle reacted with fury: "Spendthrift! Fool! Nothing proper will become of you; you are able but to waste money and to write books!" Whereupon Heine replied: "You know, dear Uncle, the best of you is that you are the bearer of *my* name."

On another occasion Heine made it known to his uncle that it was clear to him why they had chosen different professions: "My mother read belles-lettres—I became a poet; Uncle's mother read the story of the robber Cartouche—Uncle became a banker." Although the joke is poor, it was adapted to the uncle's level and hit home.

Small wonder that during the uncle's lifetime the relationship between him and his nephew was none too cordial—though Heine received from him for many years (nearly the whole of his adulthood) a monthly allowance. Heine nonetheless felt unjustly treated: in his opinion it was no more than his uncle's *duty* to provide for him.

In the poet's forty-fifth year the uncle died. His last will proved that the poet and the primitive, boastful banker who had held poetry *and* poets in rather low esteem had one thing in common: a sense of irony. The old man left his famous nephew (who had expected a round million) the sum of sixteen thousand francs. The joker in his action lay in foreseeing, as he must have done, that Heine would have his revenge by scandalizing the new owners of the family fortune. Whether the diabolical revenge perpetrated by the dying man on the living was consciously thought out remains unknown, but at any rate Heine promptly acted as expected: he started what was to become known in literary history as the "Hamburgean war of succession" (Hamburg being the family seat). The war, though fought a hundred years ago, utilized modern techniques from the arsenal of gangsters: intimidation, threats, blackmail, mobilization of the press against the family—with intimidating articles being written by Heine himself and published anonymously.

In planning his campaign, Heine concluded that the best means of frightening his wealthy relatives into coming to terms was slander, publicly planted. In a letter to a friend (Detmold) dated 1.9. 1845, he wrote:

We must work through the press for the purpose of intimidation, and the first dirt-bullets directed at Carl Heine [his uncle's son] and especially Adolf Halle [the uncle's son-in-law] shall have their effect. These people are not accustomed to that, where-as I can take whole carloads of dirt. . . . I am leaving it to your ingenuity to plant a great many little articles in journals reaching Hamburg. In these articles my uncle should be defended, and they should state that he wanted to take care of me outside of his will. They should also state that it is believed that I am in their [the relatives'] hands and am even threatened with the with-drawal of my pension if I publicly express my opinion regarding the will and the intrigues against myself. The sympathy of the public is easy to gain for the poet—against millionaires.

The enlargement of the battle order is contained in a letter written to the same friend a fortnight later:

The law suit can be used only as a threat. I can achieve some-thing [against the family; translation] only by threats. This weapon must be used quickly. . . .

Another friend (Laube) is advised in a letter, dated 11.1. 1845, to be instrumental in the journalistic double-cross:

I am forwarding two articles; let them be copied by somebody else and inserted in Leipziger Zeitung *[an influential journal; translation]. Please destroy my handwriting immediately. No. I is an attack; try to change the style in the beginning so that no-body will guess the author; the end must remain as written. . . . No. II is a defense; there is nothing to change in this one. I have written it to sound as perfidious and stupid as possible, and stylistically as bad as the usual defenses of the rich. . . . Should the editor hesitate to print the article, insert it as an ad (this is even more perfidious) and the money will be faithfully returned to you. . . . God knows I am using this art only because they are trying to cut my throat. . . .*

Heine's publisher, Campe, is mobilized too:

Carl Heine is impervious to what people say. He has but three interests: women, cigars and quiet. Could I but mobilize Ham-burg's prostitutes he would soon give in. I cannot take away his cigars, but I can endanger his wish for quiet. Here is the open-

ing in the cuirass; I shall use it. That's the purpose of the law suit; it shall serve as the framework for the tribulations I am devising. Here I can use the newspapers constantly, write memoirs, invoke God and the world, at every point letting him take the oath—no, he can't stand that and will ask me for the mercy of God to stop, before I lose the case in court. . . .

Thus vacillating between blackmail and yellow journalism, and allegedly holding his friends back from attacking the family (in articles written by himself), Heine succeeded in intimidating the family. As the price for continuation of the pension, he had to submit to censorship of all statements concerning the family. Obviously the family did not wish to pay and then be berated at their own expense. Heine summed up his experience in a letter written to his brother at the conclusion of the "war": "I can achieve more with fear inspired by my pen than by the pen itself; the great problem is to exploit that fear."

The whole incident is inexplicable without an understanding of oral-masochistic tendencies.[4]

THE SLIGHTLY PARANOIAC DEPENDEE

> *He appeared to think himself born to be supported by others.*
>
> SAMUEL JOHNSON, *Life of the Poet, Richard Savage*

Some dependees of this type have a flimsy rationalization, some do not. An example of the former is Richard Savage, described by Samuel Johnson in his well-known biographical sketch.

Savage had some unclear claim on a noblewoman, entitling him —in his own very outspoken opinion—to the title of illegitimate son. He built his life on that claim, consistently refusing to do any sort of work. Even his attempts at poetry (e.g., *The Bastard*) were for the most part a means of extorting a pension from the

[4]These excerpts constitute parts of the author's unpublished manuscript, *Heine, a Misunderstood Poet.*

woman he claimed to be his mother. He annoyed his friends to such a degree that they consented to support him by subscription on condition that he leave London. Being a classical masochistic *provocateur,* he immediately began to upbraid his benefactors, with the result that many of them withdrew their support. Savage died in prison because of an unpaid debt, although one of his friends did offer to pay the sum owed.[5]

A less elevated example, this time a clinical one, was presented by a patient of mine, a girl in the late twenties. Her wealthy father was of the opinion that his duties had ended with giving the girl a good education. On her own and faced with the necessity of earning a living, she lost one position after another by provoking her employers and by taking in general a noncompliant attitude. To make the break with her stingy father complete, she made no secret of her Lesbianism and in fact involved the puritanical old man in a number of scandals. She complained constantly of her father's stinginess, refusing, however, to adapt herself to the real situation. In her relationship with the homosexual partner she repeated the identical conflicts. She accused her girl friend of starving her by buying inadequate food of poor quality. Since she chronically lost her jobs and thus was not a wage earner, the entire burden of financing the household became the duty of the homosexual partner. Every few days there was a scene; every week a conflict. The house was in continual turmoil. In this manner the patient achieved her unconscious objective— the collecting of injustices in a never ending stream.

THE "SCHNORRER"

> *When do you suggest that I eat caviar?*
>
> A *money neurotic of the beggar type*

The untranslatable Yiddish word, *Schnorrer,* refers to a chronic beggar with pseudo-religious rationalizations, and, now a familiar word in many languages, has become a synonym for a specific

[5] For details, see *The Writer and Psychoanalysis.*

type of dependee. The Schnorrer is not a simple beggar appealing to your good heart alone; behind his supplication lies a thinly veiled impudence intended to convey that you had better comply with his wishes, or else. This mysterious or else hints at a direct pipeline to religious powers, whose deputee the Schnorrer has graciously consented to be. Privately the Schnorrer makes fun of the tricks he employs; still, as he says, "one makes a—precarious—living."

The average person is disconcerted when confronted by this type of psychic masochist, because the Schnorrer does not conform to, or even acknowledge, accepted moral standards. To heap reproaches on him is a waste of energy. His begging act has three variations: first, he tells a very convincing hard luck story; if this appeal to the lachrymal glands does not succeed in opening your purse, he turns about and impudently makes fun of you, adding a few vaguely threatening insinuations; and finally he makes fun of his own impudence, giving you as reward for your contribution at least something to laugh about.

There are innumerable jokes about the Schnorrer's impudence. One of them goes as follows: A Schnorrer extorted money from a wealthy man with the complaint that his family was starving and couldn't even buy food for the religious holidays. A few minutes later the wealthy man encountered the Schnorrer seated at a table in an expensive restaurant, eating caviar, and furiously began to upbraid him. "Look how inconsiderate you are," answered the Schnorrer. "When I have no money I can't eat caviar; when I *have* money I shouldn't eat caviar. When do you suggest that I eat caviar?"

The question arises as to why the Schnorrer manages to find contributors, when his tale is so well known. Obviously pity cannot be the propelling factor, for that very reason. The real factor is unconscious: in the Schnorrer the average human being is confronted with a living extract of masochism, naked and unabashed. The inner conscience immediately shows the prospective donor his own hidden recesses of masochism and asks ironically: "Are you really different from this man?" To counteract that reproach, there is put into operation a mechanism meant to place oneself at a distance from this incarnation of masochism. The inner alibi runs something like this: "I am different; I have only pity for so much self-destruction." The outward manifestation of the inner alibi is—a gift to the Schnorrer. The contributor pays money for intrapsychic proof that he is not identical with the Schnorrer.

**PART EIGHT: THE BARGAIN HUNTER
AND SUCKER FOR EASY MONEY**

But in the way of bargain, mark ye me,
I'll cavil on the ninth part of a hair.

King Henry IV, Part I, Act 3, Scene 1

24. A RECIPE FOR GETTING POOR QUICKLY AND EFFICIENTLY

There are many ways of throwing away money. One of the commonest, though it appears in consciousness as the *saving* of money, is that of the bargain hunter.[1]

A bargain hunter is a person who is irresistibly attracted to merchandise which he does not need but which can be bought cheaply. For a person of this type, window-shopping is not a means of orientation but an occupation full of allure. The differ-

[1] First described in "Psychopathology of 'Bargain Hunters,'" *Journal of Clinical Psychopathology,* VIII, 4, 1947.

ence between such an individual and the normal person with a normal disinclination to be taken advantage of is that for the former price is more important than usefulness, whereas for the latter usefulness and need are the first considerations.

In answer to a wife's or husband's exasperated question: "Did you need that junk?" the bargain hunter will answer with seeming rationality: "Well, I couldn't resist the price. And besides—I can use it some day." But in reality the act of buying is, for the bargain hunter, not a rational procedure but a battle of wits. He tries to outsmart the seller—who for his part is eager to give the unwitting sucker the narcissistic illusion of triumph. That many people buy for the sake of a bargain and not because of need is well known to every merchandiser; he bases his reduction sales on this fact. There are many old jokes on the subject of this human weakness; one variation has to do with a bargain hunter of antiques who happened to spy, in an antique shop, a cat lapping her milk from a saucer which he recognized as valuable. Pretending to be interested only in the cat, he bought it for five dollars and then very casually asked for the saucer, for the cat's sake. The wily dealer, also feigning naïveté, replied: "I'm sorry, but I can't let that go. You see, I'm superstitious, and that saucer has brought me luck—I've sold fifty-two cats this week."

Analysis of bargain hunters shows that they have a constant need to outsmart others. One such individual whom I analyzed managed her business badly because of her inner self-damaging tendencies. She continually grew excited over injustices done her but which she herself unconsciously provoked. She repeated in life, without knowing it, the situation of the innocent mistreated child. As a little girl she had made up a rhyme which went:

> *Mother's in the pantry*
> *Father's in the hall,*
> *I therefore put the thumbmarks*
> *Upon the parlor wall;*
> *For when the whipping's over,*
> *The pain will go away,*
> *But those thumbmarks on the parlor wall*
> *Will stay and stay and stay.*

She recited this often in adult life with such gusto that one might have suspected it was still her philosophy.

Thus she nursed the recollections of self-provoked humiliations, consciously regarding herself as an innocent victim and reacting with righteous indignation. The embalming of the childhood defeat—indeed, the constant reminder of that defeat—had the purpose of silencing the reproach of conscience: "By your naughtiness you made Mother punish you."

This woman was a classical bargain hunter and had nearly a dozen pairs of everything. Once, when buying a handbag as a present for a relative, she increased her own already large stock of handbags by a few more—because they were growing scarce.

A second patient collected virtually everything he owned via the bargain route. He spent his time haunting auction rooms.

A third patient, who was well-to-do, believed that he would be able to get even a bargain analysis. He was deeply indignant over the fee and resigned himself to paying it only after making the unpleasant discovery that his attempts to have it reduced resulted in nothing but a squandering of expensive time, especially since he regarded efforts to analyze his bargaining tendencies as sheer time-wasting. This man, having received one preliminary interpretation, left analysis after ten appointments in the vain hope of being able to do the rest of the analytical work himself. He was, as he soon found out, sorely mistaken.

A fourth patient had, at the time I knew him, shifted his interest in collecting bargains to the collection of books—and tools. He soon lost his interest in these, but admitted that bargaining for them had been a strange pleasure.

A fifth patient—a habitual bargainer—once saw a microscope in a secondhand shop window and felt that he must have it. After much haggling, he put a deposit on the microscope, only to feel guilty afterward because he allegedly could not afford it and because, as a stockbroker with no hobby in the pursuit of which a microscope could be employed, he had absolutely no use for it. His wife, to whom he constantly preached economy because of hard times, made (as he expected her to do) a good many sarcastic remarks about the useless instrument, ironically inquiring which he meant to study under the microscope: his customers' foolishness or his own.

A sixth patient, a wealthy woman, was so niggardly that she never bought herself clothes, though she indulged in constant bargaining in shops without buying. She permitted a relative to give her hand-me-downs and then complained that the relative wanted to disfigure her by clothing her unattractively. To choose and pay for her own clothes simply did not occur to this wealthy woman, except once when she happened to see an expensive dress which was being sold in one shop for a few dollars less than the same dress was selling for in another. Then she obeyed an irresistible impulse and bought the dress.

In looking for a common denominator of bargain hunting,[2] we have to exclude the possibility that the purchase has an unconscious symbolic meaning. Such a meaning may be found infrequently, and if found explains only the purchase,[3] *not* the bargain-hunting addiction. That, and that only, is hidden behind the battle of wits involved in outsmarting the seller.

We are confronted once more with a modification of an old acquaintance: the repressed masochistic wish to be *refused*. To counteract that inner reproach of the conscience, the inner defense is set in motion—the purported wish to *get*. The bargain hunter of either sex unconsciously behaves as if the outer world were but the perpetuated refusing mother. To circumvent the inner conflict, created by masochism, the problem is shifted to the act of wresting something from a hostile mother. The bargaining spirit is simply defensive pseudo aggression—*unproductively* used.

I say unproductively deliberately, because in the long run the bargain hunter is nothing more nor less than a sucker. By

[2]Bargain hunting should not be confused with "collecting." The former is indiscriminate in the choice of objects, the latter very specialized. The collector attaches an unconscious meaning to his specific predilection for specific objects.

[3]A patient of mine once started out to buy her husband a cigarette lighter for his birthday and ended up with—an umbrella. The husband had wanted the cigarette lighter and had no use for an umbrella, but the umbrella was "a better bargain." The symbolic innuendo is thinly veiled.

way of proof, all that he gets out of the *realistic* transaction is a collection of objects for which he has no use.

In addition, he either does not know or has forgotten the sound old rule: unless you are rich, you cannot afford to buy cheap, therefore poor, merchandise. And he overlooks the enormous amount of time and energy expended in acquiring those bargains that turn out to be no bargains at all.

The directly observable fact is to be recorded that the bargain hunter goes through this cycle: after having had the purchased object for a short time he becomes uninterested in his acquisition. At bottom, all that remains pleasurable is the recollection of having—as he believes—outsmarted the seller.[4]

Though a failure in the *realistic* aspect of the deal, the bargain hunter scores irrealistically, in the unconscious, some small triumph; he has purchased, for his money, a defense mechanism. In his journey into the infantile past (that past which for him is so very much alive) he denies psychic masochism and proves his purported would-be aggression.[5] He follows Iachimo's advice in *Cymbeline*: to act quickly "lest the bargain should catch cold and starve," but always finds the bargain a disappointment in the long run. In his case there is hardly any necessity to act on the cynical precept credited to the late W. C. Fields—"Never give a sucker an even break"—for he does not even give *himself* a break. He pays more than he believes for the defense mechanism against his inner masochistic attachment.

The bargain hunter has a phenomenologically different counterpart in money neurosis, a type which may be designated a sucker for easy money *without* criminal involvement. On a superficial level this pitiful individual strives for security. What

---

[4]There are many forms of haggling. The impasse encountered by the small-town bargain hunter in the large, impersonal department stores of the city is amusing. On the other hand, people who bargain with the clerk at a railroad ticket window or attempt to haggle over the price of a stamp in the post office present a problem of a somewhat different, and less entertaining, kind.

[5]Second layer of the "mechanism of orality." See Chapter 1.

he gains is—*promises* of shares, percentages, and earnings in the irreal *future* in exchange for a few thousands of *real* dollars deposited *now*. The lure of fabulous earnings is irresistible bait to this type of person, who forgets only too easily how much sweat, labor, and time went into accumulating his savings through hard work.

At once he is in a new business. The shoe manufacturer becomes a member of the board of directors of an air-transport line; the lawyer is involved in promoting a new soft drink; the physician is transformed into an angel, backing a Broadway play; and so on ad infinitum. None of these men has a trace of the specialized knowledge necessary for entering on a new venture, but, blithely discounting that fact, they confidently expect that their money investment will earn them security. And indeed they may count on security of a kind—the security of *losing*.

The excuse frequently heard is that this is solid business, with no gambling involved. This type of sucker for easy money looks with scorn on the man who gambles on the stock exchange—that "unproductive parasite"—claiming that he himself *produces*.

A taciturn and bitter-looking criminal lawyer consulted me because of general depression. His depression was, as he said, accentuated by the fact that he had not taken a vacation for years.

"Why?" I asked.

"Business."

"Don't the courts close for the summer months?"

"I said, business."

"Isn't being a lawyer your business?"

"Partly."

"Do you always speak in monosyllables?"

"Mostly."

"Why?"

"Depression."

"Will it irritate you if I phrase my sentences in the accepted rather lengthy and conventional manner?"

"Suit yourself."

"Thanks. What is the nature of your additional business?"

"Plastics."

"Do you know something about plastics?"

"The troubles."

"How did you, a criminal lawyer, happen to hit on plastics?"

"Clients."

"Whom you defended in criminal court?"

"Some."

"Some of them, or you defended them only a little?"

For the first time a mirthless smile appeared on the man's face; the smile fitted into none of his facial wrinkles and obviously was not much used. After rearranging his face into its more customary expression of gloom, he allowed a single word to escape his lips:

"Acquittal."

"Whose acquittal?"

"Clients'."

"The same clients who persuaded you to enter the plastics venture?"

"Mistake."

"Meaning you made a mistake in trusting them?"

"Ingratitude."

"Meaning that instead of showing gratitude, your clients dragged you into this venture, which you financed?"

"Talk too much."

"Who? The clients or I?"

"Both."

"Have you perhaps taken a vow of silence? Become a Trappist?"

"Through with talking."

"In court too?"

"Substitute."

"Meaning you don't go into court any more?"

"Depressed."

"Maybe you have seen too many movies caricaturing strong silent cowboys and Indians."

"Never movies."

"Stop that comedy and start talking. How did it happen that

you, a criminal lawyer, were taken in by a bunch of crooks and chiselers?"

"Security."

"Why aren't you consistent enough to use sign language instead of one-word sentences?"

"Depressed."

"I heard you before. You will have to give information or I cannot help you."

Whereupon the man dropped his pose of taciturnity, started to cry and came out with his pitiful tale. He had defended some chiselers who, through the use of some brilliant legal tricks on his part, had got off. These people then suggested that he accept, in lieu of a fee, partnership in a scheme involving plastics. The money was provided, in ever larger sums by the lawyer (the patient), who found himself becoming more and more involved. In telling his story he stressed specifically the fact that plastics actually were being manufactured and that there was no swindle connected with their production. The crookedness existed in his partners and their relations with him, and this, with the worry and excitement it caused him, had begun to be more than he could bear. For years he had been watching his investment and, in consequence, neglecting his legal work. He still hoped to regain a part of his investment. . . .

A woman in the middle thirties consulted me because someone had told her I advocated the formula, "Divorce won't help"—this being the title of one of my books. The lady mistook me to be some sort of functionary of the Court of Domestic Relations and had come to ask whether or not she had a case against her husband. After clarifying her misconception and informing her that the book title represented an abbreviation of "Divorce won't help *neurotics*" (for the reason that the "mistake" which led the neurotic to choose an unsatisfactory partner will inevitably be repeated in a second, or even a third or fourth, marriage), I explained that I am a psychiatrist. Delighted, the lady exclaimed: "That's even better than I expected—you're the very man I want. I need a psychiatrist for my husband."

"What's wrong with him?" I asked.

"He is half crazy with worries," she said, adding: "Completely unnecessary worries!"

"What is his profession?"

"That's the point. He's a certified public accountant and earns good money. But instead of being satisfied, the fool invested in some crazy new invention—cinder blocks. He needs more and more money and now he wants to mortgage our home. Fortunately, the house is in my name, and I refused to sign—I have to protect myself and my children. He does nothing but dream and worry about his crazy cinder blocks—he talks, breathes, and sweats cinder blocks, and of course neglects his only real source of income, the C.P.A. business. We never take a vacation, we can't have any small luxuries—nothing! I simply can't stand it any longer."

"Let me talk with your husband."

The husband appeared the next day, full of indignation. He first called me Mr. Buttinski, then made a crack about my name, saying ironically: "I've come in contact with a lot of crooks who pretended to be honest, and I must say that a man who *admits* right in his name that he's a burglar at least deserves credit for originality. Maybe he's even honest, who knows? Or is it a trick to divert suspicion in just that way?"

"First," I said, "you cannot spell. Second, I permit only patients who are outraged by the fee to call me a burglar. Third, by making this pun you freely admit to being a neurotic. I treat only neurotics, and in order to argue about the fee one must be a patient. Are you a patient?"

"Did you think up that answer on the spur of the moment?"

"Instead of investigating my personality and my quickness at repartee, you'd better tell me whether your wife's depositions are true."

The bubble of good humor collapsed. Once more the curtain was rolling up on the tragicomedy of looking for security. Having saved some money, this man had decided that one couldn't get rich by being a C.P.A. and had fallen into the hands of promoters who sold him on the idea of riches through wonder cinder blocks. It turned out that the business had to be reorganized, a specialist hired; competition, it further developed, was tough. He had to put up more and more money; his life became one great big hell plastered with cinder blocks.

I asked the usual question: "How could you, a specialist at figures and account sheets, fall for these crooks you allowed to become your partners?"

"You know the human weakness for getting rich," he answered.

And so on and so on, in dreary procession. Experience is disregarded in every case; lawyer and accountant alike forgot both life and professional experience when they associated themselves with crooks and promoters; selling them the Brooklyn Bridge would have been easy. The superficial explanation was "the human weakness for getting rich." The basic deeper motive was one that sounds less alluring but actually is infinitely more so: psychic masochism.

PART NINE: FLOTSAM OF MONEY NEUROSIS

That fellow seems to me to possess but one idea,
and that is a wrong one.

BOSWELL's Life of Doctor Johnson Vol. I, p. 393.

25. MARAUDERS OF THE GREAT ARMY OF MONEY NEUROTICS

A well-known writer wrote in one of his books:[1]

There comes a point in the telling of every story where you're under the compulsion to pass from the specific to the general; otherwise you could go on forever, since all endings, like all beginnings, are purely arbitrary. . . .

This observation, which is correct, applies to every extended work, not only to novels. We too must put an end, somewhere, to our journey into

[1]Charles Yale Harrison, *Nobody's Fool*, p. 296, Holt & Co., N. Y., 1948.

neurotica aurea. The main object of this book has been not to
catch a glimpse of every theoretically possible neurotic misuse of
money matters, but to lay down general lines. For a single ob-
server this is all that is humanly possible: otherwise the job would
take on the proportions of a Sisyphus' task, the describing of all
the possible forms sand may assume under the influence of the
desert wind. There are, however, a few more neurotic types to be
mentioned here. These marauders of money neurotics are characterized by a peculiar single-mindedness reminiscent of the fellow Samuel Johnson had in mind.

THE PURSE-STRING AND APRON-STRING ACROBAT

> *Some husbands hold on to their purse strings to dis-*
> *guise their holding on to their wives' apron strings.*
>
> From the author's book *Divorce Won't Help*

In a previous book[2] I described, among others, a type of husband who holds on to his purse strings to disguise his holding on
to his wife's apron strings. The question arose in connection with
the framework of the myth of the superior male. It is my contention that the hoax of the he-man is just that, a hoax—one of the
accepted fallacies of our culture. The only people who do not
consciously believe in the myth are intuitive women—and they
have no reason to reveal that it is false. The result is that man's
weakness is woman's most closely guarded secret.

Remnants of patriarchy are to be blamed for the absurd dictum
that "it's a man's world." Women are changing the dictum rapidly,
but the illusion is maintained that man is the stronger, woman the
weaker sex.

If one compares woman's life span with that of man, it is impossible to reconcile woman's longevity with man's alleged greater
strength. The tasks of giving birth and rearing children also belie
the illusion of feminine weakness.

The psychological side of the problem presents, paradoxically,

[2]*Divorce Won't Help.*

a question that is never asked: how is the transition accomplished from the helpless boy in the cradle to the adult family provider? Whether or not the he-man likes it, he was once, as an infant, *completely dependent on a woman.* Twenty-odd years later the roles are seemingly reversed: his wife and children are dependent on the once-helpless baby, now grown up. How was the change accomplished?

There are no mysteries in psychology, only questions not yet clarified. I have attempted to fill in one of the blank spots in this sector of *terra incognita.* In my opinion, the transition between *parasitic male baby* and *active family provider* is accomplished via a mechanism described cursorily by Freud though never clinically applied: *unconscious repetition compulsion.* The tongue-twisting term denotes an unconscious mechanism forcing all of us to repeat *actively* what happens to us *passively.* The peculiar reversal has the purpose of *eradicating a wound to our self-esteem, seemingly sustained by being passively subjected to an experience,* be it pleasurable or painful. By means of this formula we reverse the roles, reducing the other person to the image of ourselves in the rejected passive role, and thus are made active once more. Freud's original observation pertained to a little girl who was forced, in spite of strong protest, to open her mouth at the dentist's. Coming home, the girl immediately played dentist with a younger sibling. A duplication of a real experience—but with this important difference: at the dentist's, the child was forced *passively* to submit; in the game which followed, the child *actively* played the dentist's role, reducing the sibling to her obviously rejected passive position.

This *unconscious repetition compulsion* seems to me to be responsible for the taken-for-granted—though actually fantastic—way in which the passive parasitic baby changes, twenty years later, into the active family provider. The technique consists of identification with the image of the *giving* mother. The child-mother game is unconsciously played in reverse: the grown-up baby acts the giving mother, with the wife reduced to oneself as recipient-passive baby. She is compensated by being given love, tenderness, kindness, understanding words, sex, money. This, however, is the situation only if everything goes well and the result is relative normalcy. If that favorable result is not achieved, masochization and stabilization on the rejection level make their dismal appearance, with even more dismal consequences. The boy wards off this inner masochistic allure by unconsciously creating inner defenses. These inner defenses consist—as usual in psychic masochism—of pseudo aggression. The child in the adult then unconsciously acts the *bad, refusing mother* of his infancy, reducing his unfortunate wife to himself as baby victim. Since all this is below the level of consciousness, what we see is a mean refuser—of words, understanding, sex, and, last but not least, money.[3]

Many women, when first confronted with the baby in the man theory, have reacted in an emotional manner.

One group asserted that the whole idea was incompatible with the accepted idea of equality in marriage. When it was pointed out that they were confusing consciousness with the inherent difficulties in man's unconscious make-up, they simply repeated that the idea was abhorrent.

A second group accepted the baby in the man with a rather superior smile ("Of course I've always known it"), declaring that the baby in their respective husbands was cute and lovable, but refused any serious discussion of the reasons.

A third group behaved as if a top secret had been let out of the bag, became furious, and told me in effect: "Certain things shouldn't be discussed."

A fourth group was emotionally upset and quite unable to reconcile the two mental pictures of man—as hero and baby. They confessed that the two ingredients corresponded to fact, but were nevertheless confused by the idea.

A fifth group—mostly neurotic aggressive career women—ac-

[3]The process, simplified here to mere outlines, with many deliberate omissions, is, of course, far more complicated. It goes through a series of intermediary phases; for the scientific basis and development of the idea, first sketched in 1933 in *The Breast Complex in the Male* in collaboration with L. Eidelberg, *Internationale Zeitschrift f. Psychoanalyse*, see my book, *The Basic Neurosis*. The consequences for man's potency are far-reaching the moment the *bad*-mother-game is re-enacted.

cepted the idea gleefully and tried to misuse it in their neurotic aggression against men.

Obviously, emotional dynamite is involved in the problem, for women; that men in general disliked the whole idea intensely need hardly be said.

Still, the correctness of a hypothesis can best be checked by the number of hitherto unclarified factors that can be explained on the basis of the new assumption. Here are some of these ex-riddles:

The assumption elaborated upon above explains the ridiculous *superciliousness* of the typical man toward women: he is never heard to say, "He's only a man," but "She's only a woman" is one of his favorite phrases.

It clarifies the vociferous fight against, or grudging half ac-ceptance of, *woman's equality*. Behind conscious unwillingness to accept women in their own right lies hidden a simple fear that the *pseudo* superiority of the man who is thus being cheated out of male prerogatives may be debunked.

It makes clear why the typical man is of the opinion (ex-pressed or unexpressed) that his wife is a *sponging parasite* for whom he works himself to death. It is simply a rejection of his own parasitic baby role in defensive projection.

It answers the question of why *housework* and cooking are *deprecated as humiliating;* although they constitute a full-time job, the typical man belittles them contemptuously. The reason, once more, is unconscious rejection of the original nutritional dependence.

It sheds light on the man's behavior when he has been given *orders by a doctor* to abstain from excessive smoking, overeating, too much exercise. In many families, the wife takes over the job of enforcing these orders. What happens? The man drinks behind his wife's back, smokes in secrecy or eats what has been forbid-den when she is not watching. In other words, no adult acceptance is observable; the man indulges in infantile cheating of the image of the mother, as if it were *his wife* who had ordered abstention from harmful excesses.

Finally, the whole neurotic *approach to money* can be clarified: the weakling who is invisibly chained to his wife's apron strings takes revenge by holding on to his purse strings.

The husband who is a neurotic miser causes his wife a good deal of suffering. I am reproducing part of a discussion with a patient married to such a man:

"I always have the impression," she said, "that you are defending my husband by explaining his stingy and withholding attitude toward me."

"Correction, please. *Explaining* an unconscious tendency is not *excusing* that tendency. What good does your attitude do? You simply say 'He is a stinker'—and there the matter rests."

"But he *is* a stinker! No other word describes him so perfectly, even though it may not be ladylike. Can I help it if his miserly attitude brings out the coarse streak in me?"

"Terminology is unimportant. What is important is that you explain nothing by repeating, parrot-like, that his attitude 'stinks.'"

"I don't want to explain him, I want to change him."

"That you cannot do. He is emotionally sick and needs therapy."

"He'll never consent to that. He considers his stinginess the most natural thing in the world. That's what's maddening about it—he makes *me* look like a golddigger. If I ask for the barest necessity, he acts as if he were being highjacked."

"On the other hand, you admitted that you have often observed your husband's inner insecurity—for instance, in letting you decide important issues, even though he pretends afterward that the brilliant idea was his."

"That's even more maddening. I can't refrain from saying to myself, 'Look at this baby!' Yet the moment money enters the picture he acts like a malicious big shot. Figure *that* one out for me."

"I have done so, by explaining to you the 'baby in the man.' You just don't want to listen."

"I hate this dragging in of diapers and swaddling clothes. A man is a man!"

"You are mistaken. A man is inwardly also a baby. The fact that you cannot reasonably manage the babyish part of your husband is partially your own fault. Remember what Kipling said:

'The silliest woman can manage a clever man, but it needs a very clever woman to manage a fool.' The observation is correct, although the ability to manage has nothing to do with cleverness, only with psychic health."

"Now you will prove to me that it's *my* fault!"

"Partly. Although you informed me that you detest the psychology of diapers and swaddling clothes, the fact remains that your instinct did not warn you against associating yourself with a severely neurotic man. It is your own psychic masochism that accounts for it. Therefore you resent every attempt to explain your husband's neurotic attitude toward money. It could deprive you of your own defenses; more, it could make you see why you consider yourself such an innocent victim."

"I resent that. I *am* a victim."

"Yes and no. At best you are a fifty per cent partner in crime. There are no innocent victims in marriage. The proof that you are not entirely a victim lies in the fact that you *chose* a neurotic as a marriage partner."

The handling of money matters in marriage is a good example of misuse of irrational conflicts and expressing them in dollars. It holds true both ways: not only are there men with an irrational approach to money, but women as well. The type of demanding, sponging, constantly dissatisfied woman is too well known to need elaboration. Neurosis is not a male prerogative.

RETIREMENT NEUROSIS

> *The slaves cannot understand the free.*
>
> A patient afflicted with *"retirement neurosis"*

The term "retirement neurosis"[4] denotes a specific neurotic disease characterized by these symptoms:

[4] Described by myself in collaboration with Dr. Olga Knopf in 1944 in our study "A Test for the Differential Diagnosis between Retirement Neurosis and Accident Neurosis," *Journal of Nervous and Mental Diseases*, Vol. 100, pp. 366–80, 1944.

A *young* and organically *healthy* person consciously concentrates all of his energy on achieving an independent income at a young age—the twenties or early thirties, subordinating all other interests to that goal. The desire for retirement is not influenced by special predilections in the use of free time. *The goal is purely negative:* to be undisturbed in doing nothing.

In strange contradiction to the exaggerated expectation that the true enjoyment of living should start with an independent income is the fact that the person of the type we have in mind has pronouncedly modest financial ambitions. He is satisfied with a *relatively small income,* but one which is not dependent upon work.

After achieving his retirement paradise such an individual *does not know what to do with his time,* does not enjoy his leisure; on the contrary, sinks more and more into neurotic *depression* or hypochondriac symptoms.

If the independent income or pension is withdrawn (through bankruptcy or inflation), this person is *incapable of making a new start* and remains a failure.

A special subtype is found in the young man who inherits money and has only one occupation—to enjoy life. Even the layman can recognize that this individual is neurotic in a specific way, as is proven by the fact that the layman often remarks that work is what he needs to make him well. Such a neurotic is utterly convinced that he could not earn a dollar; he is very miserly and lives in a constant fear of social changes which might endanger or diminish his income.

With but few exceptions the person suffering *objectively* from retirement neurosis does not feel sick *subjectively.* In other words, the presence of the retirement neurosis is not acknowledged consciously; quite the contrary, the objections stemming from the outer world are consciously discarded, in spite of the fact that an *inner* feeling of guilt is present. A patient of this type enters analysis—if at all—because of other symptoms, seemingly not associated with his retirement neurosis.

As can be seen from these conditions, we are not speaking about people who retire for reasons of health or invalidism. Nor do we have in mind old people who, after many years of work, want peace and rest. We have in mind exclusively organically healthy individuals who have in *youth* a psychology which, if encountered in the late years of life, would be considered normal.

One of the cases of retirement neurosis which I analyzed twenty years ago is especially suitable for the demonstration of money neurosis and the ingenuity of money neurotics. This female patient utilized a specific social setting not encountered in other countries: she was Austrian, and in pre-Hitler Austria it was possible for an employee of the government or a large corporation to *retire with a small pension after ten years of service, independent of the state of health.* My patient devoted her life to achieving that goal.

This young woman of thirty-two entered psychoanalysis because of "frigidity, depression, sleeplessness, and personality difficulties, showing up in always choosing the wrong man," to quote her. She was—at the age of thirty-two!—a retired employee of a Viennese bank, having started her career at the age of nineteen and retired with a small pension after ten years of service—on the first day upon which that pension could be attained. All her life, she asserted, she had wanted to be independent. She had chosen her career in a bank purposely in order to retire after ten years with a pension. She endured the "hell and boredom of working" consoled only by the knowledge that one day—at thirty—she would be free to do as she pleased. She achieved her goal and retired with her small pension bolstered by a small sum which she had managed to save during her slavery, as she now called her ten years of employment.

To her amazement, the new life did not work out so well. For the first few days she enjoyed the fact that she no longer had to live under the tyranny of the clock; she could stay in bed as long as she liked; she could eat at unconventional hours and sit at the window observing passers-by. She felt superior to her colleagues, who made fun of her retirement, considering them silly slaves. But very soon she felt depressed; she attributed this, however, to difficulties of adjustment. She postponed the expectation of happiness for a few weeks, hoping that the adjustment period would pass. Time went by, but her sense of boredom and depression merely deepened. She was surprised that, in her ten years of work, she had made no definite plans on how to spend her free time. Her only thoughts on the subject had been negative ones: *not* to live by the clock, *not* to be forced to get up in the morning, *not* to have to rush to the office, *not* to waste time on boring work, etc. There were only two positive ideas connected with her plan: to sit in a chair indulging in daydreams and to read as much as she liked. Both bored her now, to her amazement. She enlarged her program and decided to regulate her sex life. She had previously had a few sexual experiences, always avoiding marriage. According to her, all of her male friends were pigs, wanting only sex without tenderness. She had retired from sex a few years before her retirement from work, having become disgusted with men. Shortly after her retirement, though, she met a young man who seemed to conform better to her ideals of tenderness. She was hit squarely in the face when this man, too, left her, saying she was frigid and yet sexually sponging. This experience and the complete emptiness of her life were the outward reasons for her feeling of being sick. She consulted the physician of her health insurance company, who consented to pay for psychoanalytic treatment for four months. She was sent to me and started treatment.

Conflicts[5] arose immediately in the analysis with regard to the time of her appointments. Since the appointments began and ended at precise times, it was up to her to be punctual. However, she always came late, though she had no occupation, cutting the appointment in half or sometimes appearing for only five minutes.

---

[5]For an understanding of the case, and many other examples mentioned in this book, it is necessary to keep in mind that psychoanalytic treatment offers a unique possibility of finding out the infantile conflict. Our conclusions are not based on "reconstruction" only, as the layman may assume, but on *specific emotional* attitudes which the patient repeats, as on a movie screen, on people actually uninvolved with the original conflict—in this case, the physician. These unconscious emotional repetitions are called "transference," and are constantly contrasted with objective reality by the physi-

She claimed that her coming late was a neurotic symptom in itself, and was furious because the analyst refused to make allowances for her tardy arrival and closed the session at the appointed time. Even the fact that the next patient was waiting failed to convince her that she suffered no injustice.

From her family history it could be gathered that her autocratic mother was the real head of the family, her father being a weak and unimportant person. She was conscious of having hated her mother all her life and of having provoked her mercilessly, and lived in constant conflict with her. She had two younger brothers whom she also hated. She accused her mother of playing favorites with the boys; only for a short time did she have the fantasy of wanting to be a boy herself. The typical penis envy developed, leading to aggressive actions toward her brothers. After the birth of the second boy she retired completely from reality and became a precocious and omnivorous reader at the age of six! There were reasons to assume that the patient regressed orally at this point, activating an early, inwardly not rejected, libidinous-aggressive position. Her incessant reading signified: "I am independent of you, Mother; I am autarchic and 'get' as much as I want." Of course that spiteful desire to "get," the precursor of her pension mania, was not the real wish at all. It represented the defense against the masochistic wish to be disappointed. That this interpretation was correct could further be proved by the fact that the patient, in her later life, usually presented her wishes in such a way that she received only disappointments, a technique which she also acted out in the transference. She went through her school years shy, sullen, indignant, often experiencing conscious hatred for everyone. She left home at nineteen, did not

cian. Psychoanalysis does not create these unconscious repetitions; they are part and parcel of the neurotic instrumentarium. The neurotic uses "transference" constantly and exclusively—it constitutes his one and only emotional tie. The difference between extra-analytic and analytic transference is that the outer world takes it at face value, whereas the analyst reduces it by "interpretations" to the infantile situation, using it as the vehicle for cure. By the same token, he is, of course, not responsible for the type of emotion the patient has in his "repetition machine."

want to see her family again, and lived only for her retirement fantasy.

Very little information could be obtained from the patient during her eight week of analysis, for she wanted first to straighten out the difficulties over her appointment hour. Since the analyst insisted that she come at her appointed time and the patient insisted that she could not, a stalemate ensued, especially when she refused to analyze her attitude. She was shown that she was provoking unconsciously a masochistic situation, that she wanted to be disappointed. By means of the simple device of coming too late with the excuse that she could not help herself, she was utilizing reality for her unconscious desire to be disappointed. It was explained to her furthermore that her outbursts of hatred and indignation were only a covering cloak for masochistic enjoyment. Every attempt to trace this attitude back to experiences and fantasies connected with her mother was blocked by her insistence that the problem at hand was a real problem and had nothing to do with the past. The idea that she should seek *displeasure* seemed senseless to her, since "she was not such a fool." To prove that she was definitely a pleasure seeker, she pointed out that she had spent the last ten years in seeking pleasure—by working toward a pension. The objection that her retirement at thirty was a neurotic action in itself was pooh-poohed by her on the ground that slaves cannot understand the free.

One day she proposed that she should come after the analyst's last appointment (at 7:30 P.M.) and wait. Since the analyst would be eating dinner during the next half hour, he would not be inconvenienced by her late arrival; he could analyze her after dinner. She parried the objection that even the analyst's day must end somewhere with the furious exclamation: "So you simply don't want to give in!" In the superficial layer this queer proposal showed megalomania and also that she considered herself an exception, who had to be loved. In a deeper layer it was intended to interfere with the analyst's pleasure in eating, since even she admitted that only a person who stood above the situation could accept such a proposal. Her unconscious desire was basically the wish to be refused. During these discussions she had the peculiar habit of playing with her pocket book and bankbook. This gesture was interpreted sexual-symbolically and as bribe and refusal, implying ironically: "After four months (the time allotted by the health insurance company) I can continue treatment at my own expense." She accepted this explanation gloatingly. Her tendency to refuse appeared not only in money matters; she refused, for instance, to mention dreams and fantasies or to produce free associations, when the analyst refused to give in concerning the time of the appointments. She had, of course, the fantasy that the analyst was upset over her refusal to come at the appointed time; it was obvious that she identified him with her mother.

After two months she started to look for another, more understanding analyst. She consulted approximately eight highly paid colleagues, offering each a twentieth of his regular fee although she was well informed about the fees usually paid for analytical treatment. Tearfully she asserted that she wanted to sacrifice one third of her monthly pension for analysis. All of these analysts regretted that they had no time available. After thus having proved to herself that nobody could understand her, she retired, full of hatred, from her analytic experiment.

Only a few details can be added to this sketchy outline. The patient practically refused to give material, being interested only in her real problem of arranging the time for her appointments. The idea that she was producing neurotic repetition in the transference seemed silly to her. One could reconstruct, however, that she repeated the mother situation in the transference. The mother was conceived by her to be a draining monster. What the patient did not even suspect was that she was masochistically attached to this mother, always wanting, through her provocations, to push her mother into the situation of refusing, so that she in turn might indulge in hatred toward her. Her own initial provocation was repressed. Afterward she pitied herself masochistically. To what extent her life was based on this wish to be refused was evidenced by her actions with regard to the other analysts. She made clever use of their relatively high fees for her purpose of being disappointed. She knew that one twentieth of the regular fee could not pay for an appointment. Unconsciously, she did not want the appointment; she wanted the refusal. Consciously, she wanted the opportunity to complain about the first analyst. Her aggressive front as a defense against deeper masochistic pleasure proved very effective: she never understood what was wish and what was secondary defense.

A few glimpses could be obtained into the genesis of her deep-seated retirement neurosis. In the superficial layer it represented an attempt at self-cure from childhood disappointments, an attempt to be independent of the refusing mother. She built a situation in which she seemingly exchanged the refusing mother for a giving one. But this giving mother—the bank—gave very little, barely covering the minimal necessities of life. Interestingly enough, the patient had no conscious feeling of being unjustly treated by the bank. This was explainable by the fact that she still fought with the bad mother, constructing in defense a good one who, for the sake of contrast, had to be elevated, as the real one had to be demoted. Her acceptance of so little also meant an aggression toward her mother: "You see with how little I could be satisfied." On the other hand, the bad mother was masochistically perpetuated: "She gives me so little, and that only as a reward for ten years of slavery."

The attempted self-cure failed, because it was a conscious and purely narcissistic effort to cope with something over which the patient had no control: her deep masochistic attachment to the pre-oedipal mother. She wanted unconsciously to repeat and enjoy the situation of being refused. That she got.

Her frigidity, too, was orally conditioned. With men also she repeated the game of being refused; everyone disappointed her. She was insatiable in sex; her last friend had called her sponging. She demanded continuous intercourse, was full of irony for the man who could not be an "intercourse machine." At the same time she was completely frigid. The pseudo-aggressive formula, covering deeper repressed masochism, was: She was not given; therefore she did not give. She reported having had only once a feeling of pleasure in sexual activity; this was a queer sensation of triumph after having indirectly forced the man to have intercourse for the fifth time during one night. Her thought at this time was: cutting off the penis during intercourse, through muscular contraction. Ejaculation of the man gave her special pleasure, since the idea of having drained him was near the psychic surface.

"GIFT-TOUCHY" MONEY NEUROTICS

> *Inconsistency is the only thing in which men are consistent.*
>
> HORATIO SMITH, *Tin Trumpet*

The neologism, "gift-touchy," was inadvertently created by a woman patient in describing her reactions to her birthday.

"I know I'm cranky today. You asked what's wrong, I am suffering from the aftereffects of an attack of gift-touchiness."

"Never heard the word. Can I find it in Webster?"

"I don't think so. You know what it means: instead of being glad to receive a gift, one gets indignant, peculiarly excited and disturbed. A regrettable experience. Let's discuss it. I had in mind to ask you about it."

"First tell me your reactions. Is your psychic allergy to gifts something new?"

"I wouldn't say so. It started with arithmetic, as it were. I felt a compulsion to find out to the penny what every gift I received was worth—and then, in reciprocating presents, I tried to spend exactly the same amount. Later it progressed to an aversion to receiving gifts in general. It got so bad that now I can't receive gifts at all, though I have no difficulties in buying them for others."

"On a restricted scale, with a limit of one dollar, I suspect."

"Now don't call me stingy! Are you riding your hobby horse again?"

"How is it *my* hobby horse if I'm interpreting your reactions? Do you or don't you want clarification on your gift-touchiness?"

"O.K. Go ahead."

"*Normally* gifts are harmless reminders of affection between people who really love or at least like each other. With acquaintances the exchange of gifts represents a social custom or repayment of a good turn. All this has little to do with money; money is just the means of expressing the loving or friendly attitude or the payment of a debt of gratitude. One chooses as a gift something that will be enjoyed by the recipient, and neither overspends nor counts the pennies. Under *neurotic* conditions, the money value of gifts is misused for the expression of unrelated conflicts. In your specific case, I suspect this connection: you cannot accept gracefully even a harmless gift because it disturbs your basic fallacy of being mistreated. You projected and perpetuated your masochistic injustice-collecting, stemming from the nursery, upon innocent outsiders."

"Do you mean I'm a parasite with a 'gimme' attitude?"

"Your indignation is superfluous and shows, once more, your complete misunderstanding of the A B C I have tried for months to hammer into you. No, you haven't a 'gimme' attitude, but exactly the opposite: you don't want to *get,* you wish to be *refused.* You also misunderstand the psychology of parasites. Their *superficial* insatiable wish to get is only an inner alibi for their wish to be refused."

"According to you, I *am* a 'gimme' type—for refusal."

"You got the point—once more; very likely only to forget it again. You are a refusal-and-injustice-collector. The basic fallacy on which your neurosis rests is based on the assumption that everyone is mean and refusing. This changes the defensive picture; it's not that you are a masochistic injustice-collector but that the outer world is mean. This in turn makes you an innocent victim—whereas actually you unconsciously *love* to be refused. Therefore, *if something happens to disturb your defensive picture, you get disturbed.* Gifts seem a case in point. If people treat you nicely, how can you maintain your fallacy of being mistreated? Therefore you first nullified every gift by reciprocating it to the penny's worth with *your* next gift, which, according to you, made you even. Hence nothing happened. You were given dollars, you repaid dollars, you were quits. Since, however, every neurosis is progressive, your inner conscience did not accept your arithmetical formula any longer, and you got peculiarly disturbed when receiving a harmless gift. Your gift-touchiness is simply an *attack of bad conscience*, showing you once more the basic fallacy on which your psychic masochism rests. *Dixi* and *salvavi animam meam*—I have spoken, may God have mercy on my soul."

"Quite a speech. Before you rest on your fallacy laurels, may I point out—I am also a fallacy hunter—that you did not explain why I have *no difficulty in buying gifts* for people *without the wish to be repaid.* I'm curious to know how you will get out of that contradiction."

"First, by advising you to use your intelligence pro and not con analysis. Second, by reminding you of a mechanism which you are ready to forget for the nth time. I am referring to the *magic gesture.*"

"Oh, that old trick!"

"To quote your 'it all depends on how one looks at things.' 'Magic gestures' are not outworn hand-me-downs but your attire. The magic gesture denotes, first, masochistic whimpering: 'Look how badly I am treated!' Second, your inner conscience objects to the hypocritical enjoyment of your psychic masochism, with the result that a defense is instituted: 'I'm not enjoying being mistreated; I hate my slavedrivers.' "

"May I remind you that constitutes *layer number three.*"

"Correct—with or without irony. To progress to layer four: your conscience objects to the pseudo-aggressive fake, too——"

"So do I, in the same way."

"Objection, please. You and your conscience object for quite different reasons: you, because you don't want to be debunked; your conscience, because it knows what it is objecting to. In any case, having got one more kick from your conscience, you institute your fifth and last defensive layer: 'I'm neither masochistic nor aggressive; I just want to show how I wished to be treated— kindly and lovingly.' That fifth fake layer constitutes the magic gesture—fake, because inwardly you want to be kicked; hence you choose *unimportant* people as beneficiaries. The more unimportant they are, the greater the masochistic accusation against your mother: 'I am good even to strangers, whereas *you* were bad to your own child.' That mechanism explains why you can *give* gifts."

"I'm sick and tired of that magic gesture stuff."

"Why not get tired of your neurosis? That would be more productive."

"Well, just tell me one thing: if these magic gestures were only defenses, the more I gave, the greater the inner reproaches against the upbringers would be, wouldn't they? I don't give *too* much. How is that?"

"Magic gestures are of different degrees. Some may even lead to being a spendthrift.[6] In other cases, the defense does not go all the way out and innuendoes suffice. Sometimes magic gestures are unconsciously used as inner irony. I know of a lady who sent her son's parents-in-law, on their golden wedding anniversary, a big, expensively wrapped box containing stale, broken cookies. Another patient told me that she desperately wanted a new fur jacket—and received from her husband, for Christmas, an expensive first edition of Molière which *he* wanted! And so on. Another patient of mine, although she was well-to-do, was always shabbily dressed; even her none-too-generous husband noticed it and insisted on her buying new clothes, giving her money for that purpose. She immediately put the money in the bank. Her unconscious motive was to nullify the gift, but she acted the refused child, forced to be shabbily dressed, in order to maintain her basic fallacy. Money neurosis has many masks."

"Why do you call it *money* neurosis?"

"You put the accent on the wrong word; it should be on the word *neurosis*. The whole concept of money neurosis is based on the fact that infantile neurotic conflicts, not related to money, are later, in adulthood, expressed in terms of money. Your gift-touchiness is a good example. You should be glad to receive gifts and touchy about buying gifts, since that involves spending money. Instead, exactly the opposite is true. The contradiction cannot be explained logically."

"Now I suppose you will quote yourself: 'Where logic ends, the unconscious takes over.'"

[6]See Part Five, Chapter 15.

"So I will. But I will also point out that the emotionalism and sarcasm displayed by you during our discussion prove how hard you fight for the maintenance of your inner defenses, hence for your beloved neurosis."

RECLUSE AND THE "RECLUSE-OID"

In solitude, when we are least alone.

BYRON: *Childe Harold*

The recluse is a person who arranges his life in modern society in a peculiar way: he lives fully secluded in his mansion (money is needed for this mode of life), having arranged for a regular delivery of a minimum amount of food; he never goes out and never receives visitors. Frequently the recluse of either sex is the scion of a once-renowned and wealthy family.

Another type, which may be called half recluse, is the wealthy man or woman who lives the life of a beggar in semi-seclusion; only after the death of the half recluse is it discovered that he had a great amount of money hidden away.

Neither type has ever been analyzed, hence conclusions drawn from their strange behavior are mere conjecture. It is possible that half psychotic mechanisms tangentially connected with money neurosis are contributing factors.

Analytical experience enters the picture, in a restricted sense only in the case of specific schizoid or only highly neurotic people whom one might call recluse-oids. These sick people live out their recluse tendencies either only partially or only temporarily. I analyzed two of them; because of the scarcity of clinical cases, I doubt that the conclusions are more than preliminary impressions, but I report them, with all the mental reservations necessary in such cases, for what they are worth.

The first case was that of a woman, a schizoid personality, whose chief aim in life was this:

"I would like to live in a little cell, completely isolated. The only contact with the outer world would be a little window which once a day would miraculously open; then some bread and a bottle of milk would appear by magic. That would be real happiness. I never could achieve my aims, but just once, twenty years ago when I was twenty-four, I came close to it. For a whole year I lived in a little room and left it only once every three days; later I arranged for delivery of a frugal amount of food. It was my father who interrupted that idyll, by calling me crazy and forcing me to give up the room. He was especially horrified by the dirt and disorder in the room—I didn't care. He was a banker, and of course he couldn't understand my beautiful fantasies."

Asked what her fantasies during that year of seclusion consisted of, the patient explained that from early childhood she had created the fantasy of a fairyland governed by a beautiful, though cruel, woman. (She had even given the woman a name.) It turned out that this beautiful woman was but the partly distorted, partly made harmless picture of the patient's witchlike fantasies of her mother, secondarily beautified through identification with the patient's image of herself. Thus she combined infantile megalomania with severe masochism. Compromise allowed her to act both roles: she was on the one hand the autarchic child ("a bottle of milk appeared by magic") and on the other the masochistic victim and prisoner in "the little cell." In her acting of the two roles, masochistic complaints (minimum of food, dirt, being prisoner in a cell) predominated, with a few megalomaniacal compensations fashioned after the principle of: "I do it myself." The beautification of her projected goddess was important: in one of the versions of the Narcissus myth of the man who fell in love with himself,[7] the self-lover dies of starvation, since he is so preoccupied with self-adoration. The myth preserves the infantile idea of self-love with rejection of dependence (food).

That beautification, however, in the case of my patient, served not only narcissistic purposes but cushioned in miniature the whole development of the *frightening* goddess into a *guiding* one.

Paranoiac ideas were interwoven: the recluse-oid also acted persecuted, and this persecution idea ("Poor little me") was only

[7]Hence the term "narcissim" (self-love), introduced by P. Naecke.

secondarily mitigated by narcissistic changes, thus depriving the goddess of her poisonous teeth. Still, enough remained of the original frightening characteristics to call her *beautiful though cruel.*

The second recluse-oid I analyzed was a wealthy young man who for years had led a secluded life in a studio. He had no contact with people, usually left his room only once a day to eat a meager meal consisting always of fish salad—because, according to him, it was nourishing and inexpensive. It is unnecessary to say that he was pathologically stingy, though admitting only to reasonable thrift. Here, too, masochistic elaboration of a cruel mother was at the bottom of the fantasy of seclusion ("Look what Mother did to me"). Many of his other peculiarities, which discretion forbids my describing (after successful analysis, the man became a famous artist), were fashioned after the masochistic guiding principles.

THE REFUSING GIVER

My wife has a selective memory.

Complaint of a patient

The technique of this species of money neurotic is invariably the same: confronted with a demand for money from his wife, he starts to behave like the proverbial wild man, shouting, cursing, reproaching, complaining, slamming angrily out of the house. When he has gone through the whole antic performance, he gives exactly the amount he was asked for in the first place. The inevitable result is that the wife cherishes in her recollection only the disagreeable scene and disregards the giving of the money. Thus this neurotic fosters in his spouse the feeling that he is a refusing miser. Consciously the man remembers that he gave the money, and forgets the row; the woman consciously remembers only the row, forgetting the money.

Unconsciously the situation is slightly different. The husband goes around with a good conscience because he gave freely, and when his wife reproaches him for his stinginess, as she invariably does, he feels terribly abused. This feeling is exactly what he was looking for, hence the scene before parting with the money. In short, the stage has been set, once more, by a psychic masochist.

Some neurotic women do actually drive their husbands to desperation with exaggerated and irrational demands. We are not dealing here with this situation, however, but with that of the neurotic type, the refusing giver for whom the inability to *give with grace* is typical. Whether the demand is rational or not, the identical initial refusal follows *automatically*.

A malicious patient once asked me what inscription I had ordered for my tombstone. Before I could answer that this was a problem upon which I had not spent much thought, or suggest analyzing his interest in my departure from the world, he continued: "Come on, let's reverse the situation for a change. You're always asking me what I'm thinking about; now I want you to give me your first association—and I bet it will be a quotation from one of your books."

"You'd be pretty good as a crystal gazer," I said. "If I were forced to decide the problem on the basis of free association—you know, eternity is a long time—I would choose a sentence from my book, *The Battle of the Conscience*. The sentence reads: '*Man's inhumanity to man is equaled only by man's inhumanity to himself . . .*'"

A good part of my scientific work has been devoted to ferreting out man's inhumanity to himself. In my opinion, *psychic masochism is the decisive factor in all neuroses.*[8] The gluttony for punishment is, of course, only an unconscious pleasure. Otherwise the formula holds true: *Every ounce of unconscious happiness is paid for with a ton of conscious unhappiness.*

Scientifically speaking, however, there is no reason to pity

---

[8]Summary in *The Basic Neurosis*. This is not, so to speak, a book but a time bomb which will go off in approximately one hundred years. Pursuant to the trend of thought suggested by the tombstone question of my patient, I can only express regret that I shall not be present to witness the spectacle.

psychic masochists. They enjoy pleasures—unconsciously, to be sure—that seem deeper and more concentrated than those of other mortals. We are able to deduce this fact from the consciously visible price of constant misery they are willing to pay for those pleasures. We are also in the unenviable position of being able to deduce the hidden pleasure of the psychic masochist from the amount of resistance these sick people put up, in treatment, when we try to free them from their scourge. In attempting to cure psychic masochists in psychoanalysis, one has the impression that an infantile idyll is being disturbed; the patients behave like a man sinking deeper and deeper into quicksand and frantically calling for help, but if you stretch out a hand to get him out of danger he refuses to grasp the hand, treats you like an intruder, and continues to call for help.

The *human* aspect is different. We see people making their lives miserable to a really intolerable degree; we know that external appearances are deceptive and that behind the superficial misery fantastically extensive unconscious pleasures are hidden, but man lives with his conscious self too, and that conscious self suffers.

Money neurosis is a great storehouse of suffering with many and variegated departments. Of course you cannot buy whatever pleases you from the great assortment; the choosing is done for you by your unconscious. Once burdened with the gift, you go through life holding onto it with iron consistency; then you call it a part of your personality, and if anyone complains, you assert that your viewpoint is the only sensible one. To silence the objector finally, you say rather indignantly: "You must take me as I am."

A patient once told me angrily, "Yesterday I was in a restaurant with some friends, and one of them, while ordering his beer, pointed at a beer advertisement with the slogan, 'Make Mine Ruppert.' According to you, *my* slogan should be contained in the order: 'Make mine misery.'"

"But it is not you who gives that order," I said. "The order is given by your unconscious. . . ."

PART TEN: PSYCHOPATHOLOGY OF INGRATITUDE

*If you pick up a starving dog and make him pros-
perous, he will not bite you. This is the principal
difference between a dog and a man.*

MARK TWAIN, *Pudd'nhead Wilson's Calendar*

26. WHAT MONEY CANNOT BUY

It is only fit and proper that this volume should
conclude on the subject of ingratitude. For in our
society the one commodity, above all others, that
money is supposedly capable of purchasing is gratitude. In all probability more time is devoted to the
acquiring of this elusive human emotion than the
results warrant: the giving of money, the lending of
money, the purchase of gifts, formal parties, formal
dinners, allowances, remittances, and on and on ad
infinitum. Even the dying attempt to reach back into
the past and outward into the future with gifts and

wills, codicils and bequests, clauses and subclauses, all the legal phraseology by which gratitude is supposedly engendered. All in all, the effort and energy devoted to the seeking and giving of gratitude is monumental.

Fortunately or unfortunately, according to the manner in which one views it, money *does not* and *cannot* buy gratitude. Nothing can buy it. The subject, itself, in all its neurotic implications, is larger than the subject of money. For gratitude, in the pure meaning of the word,[1] is encountered only as often as one encounters normalcy.

A constant source of indignation stems from human ingratitude, and every complainer has a stock of favorite examples of it. The conclusions about human nature which are generally drawn from these examples are either moralistic, pessimistic, or resigned. Strangely enough, few people ask themselves whether gratitude does not surpass human capacity, and what are the psychologic reasons for gratitude or the lack of gratitude.

Gratitude as a moral requirement presupposes that human beings react logically, the reasoning being: "I did you a good turn; you have to act accordingly." The one point overlooked in this somewhat naïve approach to the problem is the fact that gratitude has an affective case in history. It has a genetic record.

The baby, and later the young child, does not feel gratitude for food, loving care, attention and gifts, since he misjudges reality in the most amazing way. His yardstick is his own megalomania. Freud and Ferenczi have advanced the idea that the child learns only gradually to distinguish between his own body and the outer world. Consequently he regards everything good coming from the outer world, not as such, but as a gift he gives himself. According to his fantasy, only the bad refusal comes from the outside.

Gratitude has, therefore, a bad start. But the adult forgets only too conveniently his own early youth. If he remembered, and remembered correctly, he would see the picture quite differently. He would recall that he took everything good for granted, that

[1] For details see "Psychopathology of Ingratitude," *Diseases of the Nervous System,* 1945.

he considered every denial (necessary as it might be, and even for his own good) as a terrible injustice.

Every educator knows that gratitude (and decency in general) is something that must be taught to the child. Gratitude as an inborn drive is clinically not observable. What is seen clinically, however, is a difference in the success of the effort to teach expression of gratitude.

We expect from a cultured, decent human being that he feel gratitude toward his benefactor. The fact that grateful people do exist proves that pedagogy is not so hopeless a task as some pessimists assume. Parents are capable of building the feeling of gratitude in the child by making it a moral dictum. Since the child identifies with his parents he can, if he is fairly normal, restrict his original feelings that everything done for him is to be taken for granted and even show gratitude. In other words, the ability to show gratitude is an artifact built up *after* overcoming early misconceptions. It is a part of the adaptation to reality.

One of the necessary weapons of education is restriction. If the child interprets this restriction as malice (the more neurotic the child the more likely he is to do so) he acquires a feeling similar to that which a patriotic Frenchman had toward the Nazi invaders of his homeland—that everything is permissible against the aggressor. If one objects that the example is absurd, since there is no possible comparison between loving parents and barbaric brutes, the answer is that unconscious misjudgment of reality is one of the basic neurotic symptoms and signs. One cannot argue with a neurosis on logical grounds, especially since the child projects his own aggression onto his parents. The witch of fairy tales, who eats children, is a product of this conception. Neurosis is basically an anachronism; the repressed part of the personality governs. No neurotic is as old, unconsciously, as his birth certificate indicates; in unconscious development he has remained between the ages of one and three.

All educational restrictions concerned with libidinous and aggressive wishes lead the child to feel frustrated, with the resultant feeling of hate. He has only two ways out of the dilemma: identification with his educator, or unconscious continuation in a disguised form of the old slave revolt at the price of suffering. Choice of the former way results in normality; of the latter, in neurosis. This neurosis is seen clinically in differing types and specificities dependent on the genetic level of the fixation or regression.

It is the child in the adult who prevents gratitude. It is the child in the neurotic grownup who is accountable for the direct acts of aggression and meanness with which some persons repay their benefactors. Clinical experience proves that it is really dangerous to be nice to some people; they immediately repay such treatment with some mean trick, and this is all the more remarkable because previously they showed only indifference. The explanation of this seeming enigma is that the benefactor, by his kind deed, enters the magic circle of the patient's neurotic repetition compulsion. The neurotic then uses him unconsciously as a hitching post for the repetition of injustices allegedly experienced, and seeks revenge on him. The fact that the accidental benefactor is not identical with the early disappointers and has himself caused no disappointment does not matter; unconsciously he is identified with the early disappointers, and hatred, real or compensatory, is heaped upon him. He is the innocent victim of the repetition repertoire of his neurotic beneficiary:

> *Now hatred is by far the longest pleasure;*
> *Men love in haste but they detest at leisure.*
>
> LORD BYRON, *Don Juan*

Two other factors must be taken into account to explain the inner aggression of some neurotic individuals toward their benefactors. First is the limitlessness of the child's desire for love and exclusive attention. The moment the benefactor is thrown into the neurotic circle of the beneficiary's past, his deed of kindness is measured unconsciously, not in accordance with real facts but with imaginary ones. His good turn is compared inwardly to the alleged lack of love, attention and kindness over which the beneficiary grieves. This debt is projected upon the benefactor, with the result that his deed becomes an *infinitesimal part payment* of an old debt. Thus the neurotic, by means of this queer form of unconscious mathematics, changes a kind act into a negligible installment on an unpaid billion-dollar obligation.

The second factor to be considered is the quantitatively different amount of unconscious self-damaging tendencies from which every neurotic suffers as an indispensable condition of his neurosis. Psychic masochists have a peculiar approach to reality. They are submissive to the stronger person but very aggressive toward the weaker. The moment the benefactor performs a good deed, he is inwardly classified as weak by the neurotic and consequently treated by him with all the aggression at his disposal. Therefore, not gratitude, but its antithesis, aggression, appears on the surface. Samuel Johnson once stated: "Gratitude is a species of justice." True, but the eminent doctor failed to mention that *unconscious* justice is regulated not by reason but by irrational feelings.

Some people are incapable of taking gracefully any kind deed or action; they can only return the kindness of any benefactor with provocation after provocation until at last the benefactor turns from them in disgust. The reason for this continual provocation is always one and the same: that when finally refused, the neurotic may have a new source for complaining, overlooking, of course, his own unconscious provocation. Some beneficiaries have convenient methods of discarding their specific benefactors —misjudging their motives is a very common device ("He did it for publicity", or "He did it to make me feel humiliated," etc.). Or, even more curiously, they believe that the benefactor should be grateful to them for giving him the opportunity to straighten out his accounts with God by doing a good deed.

Some people advance the idea that gratitude is so seldom encountered because most individuals do not wish to be reminded of their own beginnings when they needed help. This deduction is faulty. People forget their previous dependence and their bill of gratitude because they live unconsciously on the basis of the autarchic fantasy. This unconscious fantasy negates everything worth while as coming from the outside; once more we are confronted with childlike megalomania.

Instinctive knowledge of human reactions has led some philosophers to warn against expectations of gratitude. Pierre Charron once said: "He who receives a good turn should never forget it; he who does one should never remember it." And Rousseau: "Gratitude is a duty which ought to be paid, but none we have a right to expect."

But La Rochefoucauld carried the premise one step farther; he went so far as to warn against believing in gratitude even when it is shown: "The gratitude of most men is but a secret desire of receiving greater benefits." The philosopher's observation is correct, although the psychologic reasons are more involved than he suspected. For instance, we sometimes see a display of gratitude on an irrational basis. Simple people are sometimes grateful because they feel that the kind act of a person whom they consider socially above them brings them psychologically into the orbit of the higher social stratum. Via identification, they pay tribute in their gratitude—to themselves. And sometimes exactly the opposite attitude is encountered: every kind action of a benefactor on a socially higher level is made worthless by the beneficiary's inner thought of the injustice he experiences in not being on the same economic or social level.

A very special type of ingratitude is reserved for people with new ideas: the scientist, the inventor, the poet, the prophetic homo-politicus of a high level. Biography and observation alike prove that almost every great man with ideas or techniques in advance of his generation is ridiculed; indeed, he is fortunate if he is not completely ostracized during his lifetime. Gratitude comes to him only posthumously. "The public," remarked Henrik Ibsen ironically, "doesn't require any new ideas. The public is best served by the good, old-fashioned ideas it already has." Many statements by scientists, humorists, and educators bear out this observation. Sir William Osler complained: "In science the credit goes to the man who convinces the world, not to the man to whom the idea first occurs." Donald Robert Perry Marquis remarked with some bitterness: "If you make people think they're thinking, they'll love you. If you really make them think, they'll hate you." And it was Thomas Raynesford Lounsbury who said with gentle irony: "We must view with profound respect the infinite capacity of the human mind to resist the introduction of useful knowledge."

Taking stock of the complexity of the problems involved in ingratitude and gratitude, we come to the conclusion that man has built here another of the myths by which he hides from himself. Gratitude and money seldom mix. And still gratitude is as simple as the phrase, "Thank you." And money, of course, is as simple as the phrase, "A dollar is a dollar."